Contents

2232300

List of Illustrations

RICHARD ARKWRIGHT was born in 1732, the youngest son of a poor family. His early jobs as barber, wig-maker, and innkeeper were failures, but he had always enjoyed trying to invent things. In 1775 he made a machine which not only changed the process of cloth making, but also changed the way of life of millions.

Before Arkwright, cloth had been laboriously spun and woven in the home. Arkwright's invention meant that yarn could be spun on rollers, and cloth by machines, housed in factories or 'mills', powered by water. Later, steam power made more and bigger machines possible. Britain could now produce good woven cotton cloth more cheaply than anyone else in the world. Soon all nations were buying cheap cloth from the Lancashire mills and England grew rich.

This book, by the Director of the Manchester Museum of Science and Technology, tells the story of this inventive but difficult man, constantly involved in law-suits, and almost attacked by rioters during a slump in trade. It describes the machines which revolutionized the industry, and explains how Arkwright became a knight and was able to leave his son a fortune. It contains a glossary, date chart, booklist, index and more than 50 illustrations.

RICHARD L. HILLS was educated at Charterhouse and Queen's College, Cambridge. After doing research work on Fen Drainage, he moved to Manchester to work on the history of the Textile Industry, and became the Director of the Manchester Museum of Science and Technology (now known as the North Western Museum of Science and Technology). He is the author of *Machines, Mills and Uncountable Costly Necessities*, and of *Power in the Industrial Revolution*.

Pioneers of Science and Discovery

Richard Arkwright
and Cotton Spinning

Richard L Hills MA, PhD, DIC

Director, North Western Museum of Science and Industry

Other Books in This Series

Carl Benz and the Motor Car Doug Nye
George Eastman and the Early Photographers Brian Coe
Alexander Fleming and Penicillin W Howard Hughes
Richard Arkwright and Cotton Spinning Richard L Hills
Joseph Lister and Antisepsis William Merrington
Edward Jenner and Vaccination A J Harding Rains
James Simpson and Chloroform R S Atkinson

Frontispiece Portrait of Sir Richard
Arkwright by Wright of Derby.
SBN 85078 131 0
Copyright © 1973 by Richard L. Hills
First published in 1973 by
Wayland Publishers Limited
49 Lansdowne Place, Hove, East Sussex BN3 1HF
Second impression 1980
Printed and bound in Great Britain
at The Pitman Press, Bath

Seventeenth-century design for a
spinning machine. It was probably
never made.

1 *Early Days*

The "new Piece of Machinery never before found out . . . for the making of Weft or Yarn from Cotton, Flax and Wool,"* which was patented by Richard Arkwright in 1769, proved to be one of the key inventions of the Industrial Revolution.

Many people had tried to make a machine capable of spinning a number of threads or yarns at once, but, with the exception of the silk-throwing frames, only one other person had succeeded before Arkwright. James Hargreaves, on his first spinning jenny, could spin eight cotton yarns at once. This was a great improvement on the single thread spinning wheel, yet in 1769 jennies were not very common. So cotton merchants were looking for a better machine, particularly one which could be worked by unskilled labour and could be installed in a mill where it could be driven by power.

Although his machine could easily have been worked by a single person, Arkwright realized, at least from the time of his application for a patent, that his machine had much greater potential. It was this breakthrough in power spinning, first of cotton, then of wool, and finally of flax or linen, which was so important as the launching point of the Industrial Revolution.

Because the machines produced yarn more cheaply, English merchants were able to capture a large proportion of the world market for cotton cloth. Therefore they established many more mills in England and Scotland than they would have needed otherwise. This meant that many more spinning machines, and waterwheels or, later, steam engines to drive them, and also machine tools to make them, had to be built, thus creating further demands for wood, iron, leather, bricks, timber and so on. Of course, other inventions in iron manufacture or

* Patent 931, 15th July 1769.

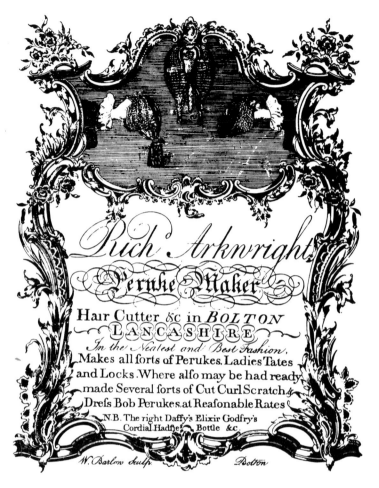

steam engine design contributed, but, through the growing export trade, the cotton industry provided outlets where these other ideas could find practical application on a far larger scale than would have been possible otherwise.

Very little is known about Richard Arkwright, and even less about the way he made his important discoveries. Indeed many people have felt that he stole other people's inventions and deny him the credit for his spinning machine. In the past, some authors have been very hostile to Arkwright, and it is therefore difficult to arrive at a true assessment of his character.

Above A woman sits spinning by her cottage door, before Arkwright's invention this was a common sight in England.
Left The trade card used by Arkwright to advertise his barber's and wigmakers business in Bolton.

He was born at Preston on 23rd December 1732, the youngest son of a large poor family. He never received any formal education or training in any technical trade and there is no account of him having any practical experience with machinery. As soon as he was old enough, he was apprenticed to a barber at Kirkham, near Preston, but moved to Bolton when he had finished his "time," about 1750, at the age of eighteen. There he was employed by a barber, Edward Pollit, and continued to work for Mrs Pollit on his master's death before setting up on his own a little later. He seems to have built up quite a successful business as a barber and peruke or wig maker, and copies of his trade card survive.

In 1755, he married Patience Holt of Bolton, who bore him his only son, Richard, on 19th December the same year. Unfortunately she died in 1757 and her death may have been one of the reasons for his business failing so that he had to leave Bolton, probably in debt. He tried to run a public house, either at the same time as he ran his barber's business or after abandoning that trade, but spent too much on the alterations and decorations and had to give up. At this time he was plagued with asthma.

The next fact we know about his life is his second marriage in March 1761 to Margaret Biggins of Leigh. It does not seem to have been a very happy union and later he left her. They had one daughter, Susannah. About the time of his marriage, Arkwright was travelling around the country buying hair for making wigs, and his wife may have provided the capital to do this. He had an eye for business even then, for somehow he obtained, or possibly invented, a way of dyeing hair which enabled him to sell it to other wig makers.

According to Stephen Glover writing in 1829 in the *Derbyshire Directory*, Arkwright was based at Wirksworth for a time before 1768, when he could have become familiar with the area where he later

Overleaf top Different ways of spinning and reeling yarn to prepare it for weaving. Spinning from a distaff (*left*) is the oldest method.
Overleaf left Handloom weaver's cottage at Delph, Yorkshire. The long windows provided light.
Overleaf right Inside her cottage a woman spins thread on a spinning wheel. For centuries this had been the only improvement on the distaff.

built his cotton mills as he travelled round the fairs buying hair. Fashions changed and the demand for wigs fell off, so he had to find some other employment. After his marriage, he was frequently at Leigh, and this was how he met Thomas Highs, a reed maker of Leigh, and John Kay, a clockmaker of Warrington, who were trying to build a spinning machine.

Arkwright himself might already have been familiar with spinning. At that time, flax from Ireland was being spun into linen in the Preston area. Bolton was also one of the first places to develop a cotton industry, for spinning and weaving cotton can be traced back before 1600. Gradually this industry expanded and drove out the older woollen trade. Doubtless the problems of the textile industry were

fig. 2.

often discussed in the barbers' shops of the town, so Arkwright would have been well aware of the urgent need for a spinning machine.

By 1750, Manchester had established itself as the natural centre of the cotton industry, supporting a ring of manufacturing towns around it, such as Bolton, Leigh, Bury, Middleton and others. At this period it seems that the greater part of the cloth produced in Lancashire was a mixture of cotton and linen. The reasons for this stretched back a long way.

The East India Company had developed a profitable trade selling printed Indian calico cloth which had assumed such proportions in this country that by 1700 it was seriously threatening the English woollen industry. After a great deal of violent agitation from the wool workers, Parliament passed an Act in 1700 putting a heavy duty on imported "Painted or Stained Calicos." This did not have the desired effect for it merely encouraged the small English calico printing industry to expand, using imported grey cloth or possibly cotton cloth.

When the wool interests realized what was happening, they petitioned Parliament again and in 1721 another Act was passed banning the wearing of any printed cloth with cotton in it except for muslins, neck cloths and fustians. The term "fustian" included a wide range of fabrics and such a trade was bound once more to arouse the hostility of the wool merchants.

In 1736, after the wool supporters had claimed that most of the cotton trade ought to be banned under the terms of the Act of 1721, a further Act had to be passed which allowed the manufacturers of Manchester to continue producing fustians if the warp was entirely linen yarn. The linen came mainly from Ireland while the cotton for the weft came mainly from the colonies in the West Indies, so British trade benefited and the Lancashire cotton industry survived. However, some taxes remained on cotton cloth, with heavier taxes on any imported.

In 1750, the whole cotton industry was based on the domestic system. The wife and older daughters did the carding and spinning, while the father and boys did the weaving. People who were too old to spin or weave would wind the pirns or quills for the weavers' shuttles. Most families owned a small-holding, so agricultural work was fitted in with textile production. The Pennine foothills are poor agricultural land, and no doubt most farmers were glad to have a second occupation to supplement their income. Gradually the dependence on the textile industry increased, particularly when the small-holding was divided between brothers on their father's death so that each plot became too small to support a family.

There were advantages and disadvantages to this system. When there was a lot of work to do on the farm, such as at harvest, cloth production was neglected. On the other hand, in a slump, the family could eke out a meagre existence on the farm and was not completely destitute. When the cotton industry boomed through the inventions of Arkwright and others, there was ready to hand a large number of part-time workers who were willing to leave their farming and concentrate on textile production.

While each household may have been at one time a free and independent unit, buying wool where it liked and selling its cloth where it could, by 1750 it is probable that most Lancashire weavers were linked up with one particular merchant. He knew what type of cloth was in demand and could instruct his weavers accordingly. The master of the household went to the merchant to collect the raw material and receive his instructions. For the mixed cotton and linen cloths he would be given the correct length of linen warp already prepared for the loom. This would have been spun in Ireland, or other parts of

Above The Great or Jersey wheel, introduced around 1350, was the first improvement made in the process of cotton spinning. Thread could be spun faster on the wheel than with the traditional distaff. *Right* Wire card making machine invented by Robert Kay, which bent and stuck the wires through the leather backing.

Lancashire such as Preston, and made up at the warehouse.

The cotton, on the other hand, was handed out in the raw state and the weaver was responsible for having it spun locally. First any dirt, seed and seed-pods had to be "picked" out. Then the fibres had to be disentangled and laid parallel to each other. This "carding" was done with a pair of boards covered with leather through which were stuck fine wire hooks or points to catch the fibres as one board was pulled gently across the other. When sufficiently loosened, all the fibres were transferred to one board and pulled off in a roll.

Over the years there had been few improvements to carding. In 1750, William Pennington had patented a machine for making holes in the leather backing through which the wires were inserted and

15

soon after that Robert Kay developed a machine for cutting, bending, and inserting the wires through the leather. Cards larger than usual were tried, called stock cards. Sometimes the lower card was firmly fixed to a table and the upper one might be suspended by a series of pulleys and weights to help take the load. Even in 1770, no one had managed to improve on this.

While it was possible to spin a thread directly from the carded sliver or rollag, for the finer cotton yarns, and perhaps for most yarns, the sliver was drawn out on one spinning wheel and slightly twisted to make a roving. The roving was drawn out on another spinning wheel and twisted into the finished yarn. There had been no improvements to spinning since the Middle Ages, and in fact all spinning methods have relied on two simple principles until the recent invention of "break" spinning.

The first principle is that if a rod or spindle is rotated, any length of string or yarn tied to it and held in the same line as the spindle is pointing will be rotated too and so will be twisted. The yarn will still be twisted if it is held at an angle to the spindle for it will wind itself in a spiral along the spindle until it reaches the end when it will flick over the top and again will be twisted. This twist binds the loose fibres together and transforms the spongy carded sliver into a firm length of yarn. The second principle is that if the yarn is held at right angles to the spindle, it will be wound on.

The woman, spinning with her simple spindle, used these two principles. After knotting the yarn to the top of the spindle, she prepared to spin the next length by setting it rotating. With her fingers she pulled out the correct number of fibres from the sliver to form the right thickness or weight of yarn and then allowed the twist from the spindle to bind them together. In this way the piece of yarn gradually lengthened and the spindle descended towards

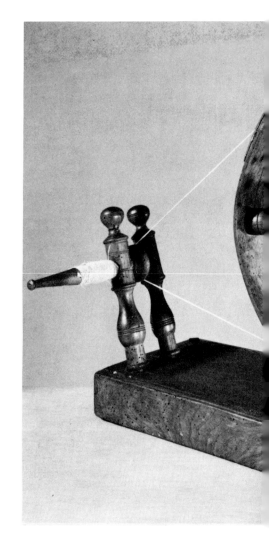

After their introduction in the fourteenth century, spinning wheels came in a variety of sizes and styles. This small table wheel, dates from c. 1600.

the ground. A circular weight or "whorl" gave momentum and helped to keep the spindle turning, but from time to time the spinner had to give another twist to keep it rotating. When it had nearly reached the floor, she had to untie the knot and wind on the new length.

All wool, flax and cotton was spun like this from prehistoric times until about 1350 when the great or Jersey wheel was introduced. This had a large wheel with a flat rim round which a band passed to a small pulley on the shaft of a horizontal spindle so this revolved many times faster. In her left hand, the spinner held the mass of carded fibres which she pulled away from the spindle, paying the fibres out through her fingers and putting the twist in at the same time by turning the large wheel with her other hand. The yarn left the spindle at an angle and it was possible to spin a length of about six feet before it had to be wound on.

To spin evenly and consistently demanded considerable skill, for the quality depended upon the feel of the fibres passing through the fingers and also on putting in an equal number of turns each time. To wind on this length, the wheel had to be turned backwards to unwrap the spiral coils from the top of the spindle. Then, with the yarn held parallel to the wheel and at right angles to the spindle, the wheel was turned in the original direction and the yarn reeled up in a nicely shaped cop.

To mechanize this complicated system of spinning and make it automatic must have seemed almost impossible, yet these were the principles James Hargreaves used on his spinning jenny, followed by Samuel Crompton on his mule, which was originally invented in 1779 and was finally made to work automatically in 1835. This method has always suffered from the fact that the spinning and the winding are entirely separate phases involving different actions, so that spinning is comparatively slow. In addition, the spinning jenny suffered from further defects because it was awkward to use and needed a skilled person to operate it efficiently. Finally, the yarn which could be spun on it seems to have been fairly weak so it was unsuitable for many varieties of cotton cloth.

The other type of spinning wheel, called the flax or Saxony wheel, was introduced around 1400 and must have seemed far more promising for mechanization. As in the great wheel, a band round a larger wheel also turned the spindle, but in this case, the large wheel was turned by a foot pedal, leaving both hands free to pay out the fibres. On the end of the spindle nearest the spinner a horseshoe-shaped "flyer" was fixed, while the spindle pulley could be unscrewed to allow a bobbin to be slipped onto the spindle shaft. This bobbin was driven by a second band and had a different sized pulley, so that it rotated at a different speed from the spindle and flyer. As the spinner paid out the fibres, they were twisted by the rotation of the spindle.

The spun yarn passed through a hole in the end of

the spindle, thus completing the first of the spinning processes. To bring the yarn to a right angle with the spindle so it could be wound on, it was passed round a hook or heck on one of the arms of the flyer from where it was pulled onto the bobbin. The rotation of the spindle gave the twist, and the slight difference in speed of the bobbin and the spindle gave the winding on, so both were happening continuously together. Wool and linen could be spun on this type of wheel but rarely cotton, because its individual fibres are too short.

Arkwright may have been familiar with this type of wheel from his childhood in Preston and, from its continuous action, it was the obvious type to try and mechanize. If some mechanical action could be found to copy that of the spinner's fingers, then the Saxony wheel would form a good basis for a spinning machine.

Indeed, a variation of the spindle and flyer had been used in Italy for silk "throwing" since at least 1500. There were no drawing or drafting problems with the long silk filaments so the strands of silk merely had to be twisted together. First they were wound on to bobbins which then were placed vertically in large machines with the flyers set above them. The flyers were rotated and the silk drawn off through them so the filaments were twisted together. The bobbin was not driven but rotated a little slower than the flyer because its own weight caused friction against the ledge on which it sat, thus retarding it.

Thomas Cotchett tried to build a waterpowered mill with silk-throwing machines at Derby in 1702, but he failed and it was left to the half-brothers Thomas and John Lombe to establish the first successful power-driven English textile mill for throwing silk in 1717 at Derby beside Cotchett's earlier site.

Although there had been no other improvements in carding and spinning, advances had been made

Opposite The Saxony wheel, a more sophisticated version of the Great wheel, introduced about 1400. The wheel was worked by a foot treadle, leaving both the spinner's hands free to work the thread.

Opposite With the Industrial Revolution and mechanization, the cotton industry moved from the workers' homes to great factory sheds. Here, in 1835, mules spin many hundreds of cotton threads at once.

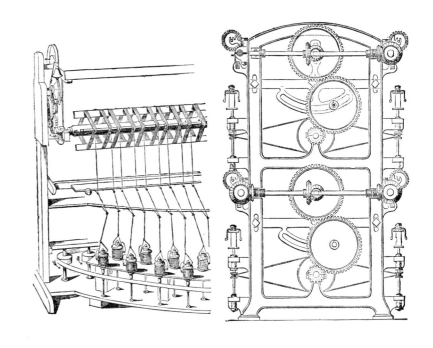

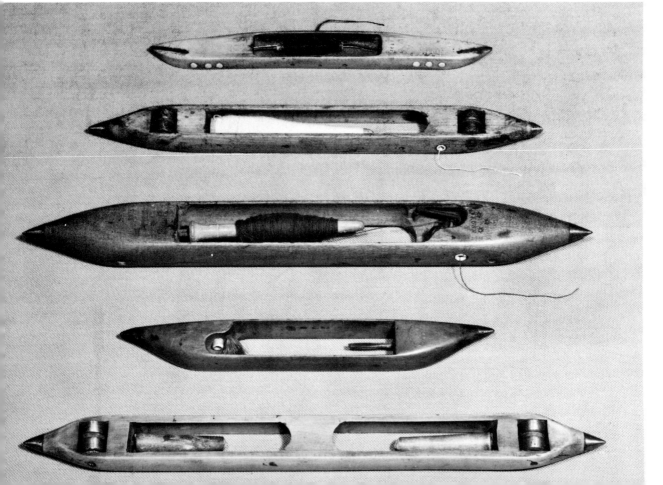

Above A manually operated stocking knitting machine.
Opposite top Machinery for throwing silk thread. The first successful power-driven silk mill in England was established at Derby in 1717.
Opposite below Types of flying shuttle. Shuttles 2, 3 and 5 (from the top) were invented by John Kay around 1733, it was not widely used until nearly thirty years later. They helped increase the speed at which cloth could be woven.

in both weaving and knitting. During the eighteenth century, various mechanisms were invented for weaving more and more complicated patterns. Most of these originated in France and culminated in the machine which Jacquard first exhibited at Paris in 1800. These devices made looms more versatile and helped to cheapen patterned cloth production, so increasing the demand.

More important to the story of Arkwright are the inventions of the Englishman John Kay and his son Robert. In 1733, John Kay, who was no relation to the John Kay known to Arkwright, patented his flying shuttle. At either end of the reed on a loom, he placed a box in which the shuttle could be caught after it had been sent through the warp, leaving a trail of weft behind. Sliding above each box was a device like a hammer which could be pulled to send the shuttle back through the warp. The hammers were attached to a central picking peg which was worked by one hand while the other beat up the weft with the reed.

The speed of weaving could be doubled with the flying shuttle but this invention does not seem to have been used very much until Robert Kay developed the drop box around 1760. Three or four shuttles with wefts of different colours were stored in separate boxes, one above the other, and selected whenever the weaver desired. This considerably increased the speed of weaving multicoloured cloth and brought flying shuttles into general use. Their big disadvantage was that they were useless unless there was a plentiful supply of yarn, but cloth could be woven more quickly by them.

Knitting also had been greatly improved during this period. In 1589, the Reverend William Lee invented a knitting machine which although gradually improved, could only be used for plain knitting. No improvement took place until 1759 when Jedediah Strutt in Derby produced an attachment

As recently as 1971, this old-style jacquard hand loom, complete with flying shuttle and drop boxes, was being used to weave silk ties at Macclesfield.

for making ribbed knitting. This unleashed a series of further inventions which enabled a variety of stitches, net, and even a sort of lace to be made on the original frame.

These new varieties increased the demand for yarn which, together with the increase on the weaving side, precipitated a crisis because all wool, cotton and flax still had to be spun on the single thread medieval wheels and the supply of yarn was inadequate.

It is difficult to estimate how much yarn one weaver needed or how much one spinner could produce because spinning and weaving the finer counts took much more skill and time. Different writers give various estimates of the number of spinners required to keep one weaver at work, ranging from four to eight or even ten or twelve. Often no indication is given whether these people were working full or part-time. If, as a rough average, we assume that about eight spinners are needed per weaver, the weaver's difficulty in securing regular supplies of yarn or weft will be realized.

Some accounts of the period around 1760 say that weavers had to walk many miles to find spinners and then they had to give them presents or a high rate of pay to have the yarn ready in time for the cloth to be woven by the end of the week. Often the spinning was done badly, the yarn being lumpy and irregularly twisted. Under these circumstances, it is not surprising that many people were trying to invent a satisfactory spinning machine.

2 *The First Patent*

The people who came nearest to inventing a successful machine for spinning cotton before Hargreaves and Arkwright were Lewis Paul and John Wyatt.

Their machine had spindles set round the circumference of a circle with a large horizontal wheel in the middle turning all of them. The spindles had flyers, while the fingers of the hand spinner were replaced by a pair of rollers or cylinders. The cotton sliver from the stock cards was laid on a strip of paper and wound round the upper cylinder. This rested on the lower which was also driven by the horizontal wheel. As the cylinders turned, the cotton was paid out between them and the paper was wound on to the lower one. The fibres were meant to be drawn out by the pull of the flyer and bobbin, both of which were driven by gearing, and the twist was put in at the same time. This seemed to copy the action of the hand spinner.

While cotton fibres are being drawn out, they must be free to slide past each other or they will stick and break. But if there is nothing to hold them gently together, they will fall apart and separate. Therefore there must be a little twist, but not so much as to prevent the fibres from being drawn out to the right thickness. The hand spinner can feel how much twist she needs to put in and if necessary can put in more after she has done the drawing. This cannot be done on a machine with the spindle and flyer because the twist runs up the yarn to the nip of the rollers where the fibres are being paid out and binds them firmly together there.

Paul and Wyatt tried to draw out the fibres between the rollers and the flyer and failed because the drawing or drafting stage must be kept separate from the twisting or spinning stage on this type of

machine. Either their finished yarn would have been too lightly twisted to have any strength, or, when they tried to get a firmer twist, they would have had many breakages because the fibres would have locked themselves together and would not have drawn out. They conducted a great many experiments between 1736 and 1745, and Paul continued trying until 1758. They established waterpowered mills at Northampton and Ludlow, but, in spite of considerable promise, their machines were failures because they were using the wrong principles.

In 1761, the Society for the Encouragement of Arts, Commerce and Manufactures offered a reward of £50 for a successful spinning machine. Various people tried to make machines, for example Thomas Earnshaw of Mottram, or John Taylor, who took out a patent. One day a spinning wheel in James Hargreaves' home was accidentally knocked over. As it lay on its side, still rotating, it inspired him to try making a machine.

When spinning with the great or Jersey wheel it is possible for the spinner to grasp firmly the sliver or roving leaving three or four inches of unspun fibres between the fingers and the spindle. Her fingers, still tightly clamped, are pulled away from the spindle, drawing out the fibres. If the spindle is rotated gently at the same time, the fibres will cohere together as they are pulled out. The roving can be drawn out into a fine yarn because the twist runs into the thinnest places first, binding them together, while the thicker parts are more loosely twisted and so can continue to be drawn out. If the spinner does not twist enough, the yarn disintegrates, while if she twists it too much, she locks it together before it is drawn out fine enough. When it is fine enough, she must put in more twist to hold it all firmly together, and then she can back off and wind on in the usual way.

To spin like this requires a very sensitive touch and would seem impossible to mechanize, yet it was this method which Hargreaves used on his jenny. He placed the spindles at the far end, slightly inclined from the vertical towards the spinner. They were driven by bands from a large wheel turned by the right hand. Instead of his fingers, he had a sliding wooden clamp to hold the eight rovings he spun on his first machine. The left hand drew the clamp back as the yarn was being spun and pushed it forward to wind on.

It was always a difficult machine to operate because great skill was required to coordinate the twisting, drawing and winding. It was easier to use with the longer fibres of sheep's wool and survived in the woollen industry long after it had disappeared from the cotton. However, it did ease the problem of weft supply, for even on the small early machines, one spinner could provide enough weft to keep one weaver at work. By 1770, its size had increased to sixteen

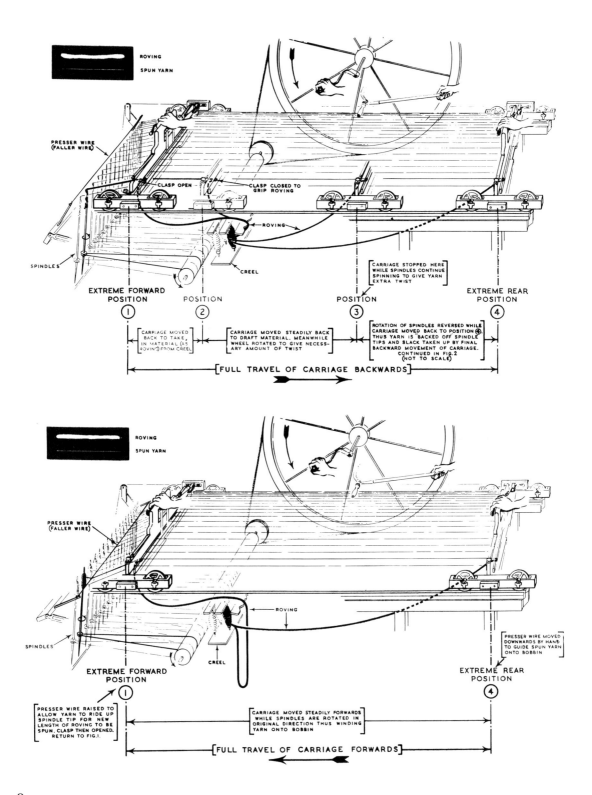

ROVING

SPUN YARN

PRESSER WIRE
(FALLER WIRE)

CLASP OPEN

CLASP CLOSED TO
GRIP ROVING

ROVING

SPINDLES

CREEL

EXTREME FORWARD
POSITION
①

POSITION
②

CARRIAGE STOPPED HERE
WHILE SPINDLES CONTINUE
SPINNING TO GIVE YARN
EXTRA TWIST

POSITION
③

EXTREME REAR
POSITION
④

CARRIAGE MOVED
BACK TO TAKE
IN MATERIAL (AS
ROVING) FROM CREEL

CARRIAGE MOVED STEADILY BACK
TO DRAFT MATERIAL, MEANWHILE
WHEEL ROTATED TO GIVE NECESS-
ARY AMOUNT OF TWIST

ROTATION OF SPINDLES REVERSED WHILE
CARRIAGE MOVED BACK TO POSITION ④,
THUS YARN IS BACKED OFF SPINDLE
TIPS AND SLACK TAKEN UP BY FINAL
BACKWARD MOVEMENT OF CARRIAGE.
CONTINUED IN FIG.2
(NOT TO SCALE)

[FULL TRAVEL OF CARRIAGE BACKWARDS]

ROVING

SPUN YARN

PRESSER WIRE
(FALLER WIRE)

ROVING

SPINDLES

CREEL

EXTREME FORWARD
POSITION
①

EXTREME REAR
POSITION
④

PRESSER WIRE MOVED
DOWNWARDS BY HAND
TO GUIDE SPUN YARN
ONTO BOBBIN

PRESSER WIRE RAISED TO
ALLOW YARN TO RIDE UP
SPINDLE TIP FOR NEW
LENGTH OF ROVING TO BE
SPUN, CLASP THEN OPENED.
RETURN TO FIG.1.

CARRIAGE MOVED STEADILY FORWARDS
WHILE SPINDLES ARE ROTATED IN
ORIGINAL DIRECTION THUS WINDING
YARN ONTO BOBBIN

[FULL TRAVEL OF CARRIAGE FORWARDS]

spindles and this soon reached eighty, but it always remained essentially a cottage machine, being set up chiefly in people's houses.

Arkwright's machine was totally different. Probably we shall never know how he developed it, although the original example which he had to submit with his patent application is preserved in the Science Museum in London. From this, and the description in the patent rolls, we can see what he did but not how he did it.

He used the flyer method of spinning, and placed four spindles with their flyers and bobbins vertically near the bottom of his machine. The bobbins were not driven but were slightly retarded by light string brakes. At the top of the machine he placed the vital drawing rollers which have barely changed since.

There were four sets of paired rollers. The top roller of each pair was covered with leather, and was kept firmly in contact with the bottom roller by a weight. The bottom rollers were made from metal and wood, and had flutes cut along them. These lower rollers were connected together by gearing so that one shaft could turn them all. They did not all turn at the same speed, for the back pair, where the thick cotton roving entered, rotated slowest and each succeeding pair turned faster. In this way, the roving was drawn out until the correct number of fibres was passed out between the nip of the front rollers where the twist from the spindle locked them firmly together and made the finished yarn.

Arkwright did not have the skill to make this machine himself, so he employed John Kay, the Warrington clockmaker, to help him. Earlier, as it happens, John Kay had helped Thomas Highs with a spinning machine as well, and one story says that Kay showed Highs' machine to Arkwright who copied it and took all the credit for the invention. Richard Guest, writing in 1828, championed the

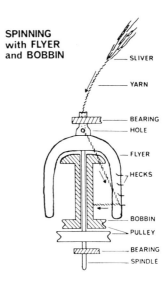

SPINNING with FLYER and BOBBIN

SLIVER
YARN
BEARING
HOLE
FLYER
HECKS
BOBBIN
PULLEY
BEARING
SPINDLE

Opposite top The drafting and twisting action of the spinning jenny. *Opposite below* The action of the jenny as it winds the thread. *Below* Arkwright's prototype spinning machine, made for him by John Kay.

cause of Thomas Highs and published a picture of his machine which looked very much like Arkwright's for it had flyers and two pairs of rollers to draw out the cotton. Paul and Wyatt also may have tried to use multiple pairs of rollers for the drawing stage, so why did they fail and Arkwright succeed?

Probably Arkwright added two vital contributions. First he realized that the different pairs of rollers must be set at the correct distance apart. While he claimed in his patent that he could spin cotton, flax and wool, in fact he could spin only cotton with the

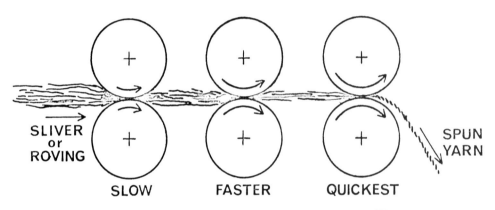

SLIVER or ROVING   SLOW   FASTER   QUICKEST   SPUN YARN

Patented by Arkwright in 1769.

The diagram shows the way in which the rollers in Arkwright's machine worked.

rollers set as they are on the machine in the Science Museum. All these different types of fibres have different staple lengths. The length of the average cotton fibre is just under an inch, while the best quality Sea Island cotton has fibres up to one and a half inches long. This will be short for most wool fibres, which may average from two to six inches in length depending on the quality and type. Flax fibres will be even longer.

Arkwright's machine was not adapted successfully for these longer fibres until worsted spinning started at Dolphinholme Mill in Lancashire in 1784, and flax came even later. If the rollers are set too close together so two pairs can grip the same fibre, this fibre cannot be drawn past its neighbours and will be broken. If the rollers are set too far apart so the fibres float between them and are not gripped by either, the drawing will be uneven and a lumpy or broken yarn will result. Ideally, all the fibres should be the same length and the rollers set a little farther apart than this length. Then there is only a very short time after the fibre has passed out of the nip of

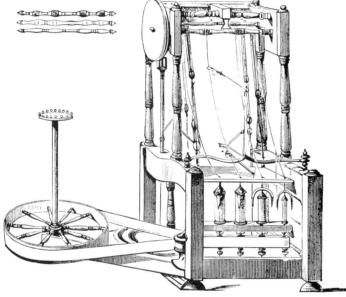

Arkwright's water frame spinning machine, patented in 1769.

the slower turning set before it is gripped by the next pair turning more quickly and thus is drawn out.

In order to hold the fibres tightly in the nip of the rollers, Arkwright made his second contribution. He hung weights on the top rollers so they were pressed hard against their lower counterparts. Paul and Wyatt did not weight their rollers and in addition do not seem to have realized the vital importance of the staple length. If Guest's drawing of Highs' machine is accurate, then Highs spaced his rollers too far apart, and did not weight them. What is certain is

31

Richard Arkwright, to whose inventiveness the English cotton industry owed so much.

that on his patent machine of 1769, Arkwright introduced these two vital features, the correct spacing of the rollers and their weighting. Without them, no roller spinning machine will work satisfactorily.

We know that Arkwright had moved to Preston with John Kay in January 1768. They had rented rooms from a Mr Henry at seven guineas per annum where they said they were "making a machine to find out the longitude."*

At about this time, Arkwright must have felt he was on the point of success and it was at this stage that his business acumen became evident. He had developed a machine which although it still needed many improvements could be operated by an unskilled person. All the spinner had to do was to see that it was supplied with rovings at the back of the rollers, to fit empty bobbins whenever they were filled with yarn and to piece up the yarn when it broke. Such a machine with its continuous action was eminently suited for a power-driven factory.

* *Palatine Note Book*, ed. Bailey, vol iii (1883), p. 263.

Arkwright could have made more machines and sold them locally, like Hargreaves had done, or he could have allowed his machines to be built on a small scale and used in cottages. Instead his business sense told him his machine had much greater potential because it could be set up in power-driven factories.

A factory required much more capital than Arkwright possessed, and his frame still needed to be perfected, so he had to search for financial help. He had to convince someone that his machine, which alone must have been quite expensive, set in an expensive mill could produce yarn cheaper than the spinner working in her home. Possibly Arkwright did not realize at this time that he would have to mechanize the other parts of cotton spinning, because the new machine spun quicker than the cotton could be prepared by hand.

Considerable investment would be necessary to make his invention a commercial success, and naturally he did not want anyone to steal it in the meantime. One way to protect himself, and also to make a profit, was to take out a patent.

If a patent was granted, the holder alone had the right to it for fourteen years. Either he could make the machines and sell them to others, or he could sell licences allowing other people to use his invention. Anybody using the invention without a licence or agreement was liable to prosecution. But patents could only be obtained by petitioning the Patent Office and money was needed to pay the legal and patent fees. Since Arkwright probably did not have enough capital to meet these expenses, he had to find some backers.

Some recently discovered documents throw a little more light on this period but do not clear up all the problems. The first shows that on 14th May 1768 Arkwright made an agreement with two people who were willing to become "Joint Adventurers and

A.D. 1769 . . . . . . Nº 931.

Spinning Machine.

ARKWRIGHT'S SPECIFICATION.

TO ALL TO WHOM THESE PRESENTS SHALL COME, I, RICHARD ARKWRIGHT, of the Town of Nottingham, in the County of Nottingham, send greeting.

WHEREAS I, the said Richard Arkwright, did by my petition humbly
5 represent to His present most Excellent Majesty King George the Third, that I had by great study and long application invented "A NEW PIECE OF MACHINERY NEVER BEFORE FOUND OUT, PRACTISED, OR USED, FOR THE MAKING OF WEFT OR YARN FROM COTTON, FLAX, AND WOOL, WHICH WOULD BE OF GREAT UTILITY TO A GREAT MANY MANUFACTURERS IN THIS HIS KINGDOM OF ENGLAND, AS WELL AS TO HIS
10 SUBJECTS IN GENERAL, BY EMPLOYING A GREAT NUMBER OF POOR PEOPLE IN WORKING THE SAID MACHINERY, AND BY MAKING THE SAID WEFT OR YARN MUCH SUPERIOR IN QUALITY TO ANY EVER HERETOFORE MANUFACTURED OR MADE;" I therefore humbly prayed His said Majesty to grant unto me, my executors, administrators, and assigns, His Royal Letters Patent for the sole making and
15 vending the said machine or Invention within that part of His said Majesty's Kingdom of Great Britain called England, His Dominion of Wales, and Town of Berwick-upon-Tweed, for the term of fourteen years, agreeable to the Statute in that behalf. His said Majesty, being willing to give encouragement to all arts and inventions which might be for the publick good, was graciously
20 pleased to condescend to my request; and therefore, by His Royal Letters Patent, bearing date at Westminster, the Third day of July, in the ninth year of His reign, of his especial grace, certain knowledge, and meer motion, for Himself, His heirs and successors, did give and grant unto me, the said Richard Arkwright, my executors, administrators, and assigns, His especial licence, full
5 power, solo priviledge and authority, that I, the said Richard Arkwright, my executors, administrators, and assigns, and every of us, by myself and them-

34

Partners'' in the spinning venture. They were John Smalley, publican and paint merchant of Preston, and David Thornley, a merchant of Liverpool. They agreed to "Advance in equal Proportions all such sums of money as might be necessary in applying for a Patent as aforesaid and for Improving, Enlarging, Using and Working the Machine already Invented and others to be constructed for the same, or the like purposes, and all incident Charges and Expenses that might attend the same . . . "*

The patent application was made in June and signed by Bigoe Henzell and John Smalley, but the patent was not granted until 15th July 1769, possibly through lack of finance to pay the fees. The

In witness whereof, I, the said Richard Arkwright, have hereunto set my hand and seal, this Fifteenth day of July, in the year of our Lord One thousand seven hundred and sixty-nine, and in the ninth year of the reign of our said Sovereign Lord George the Third, by the grace of
20   God, of Great Britain, France, and Ireland King, Defender of the Faith, and so forth.

RICH^D (L.S.) ARKWRIGHT.

Sealed, and delivered (being first duly stamp), in the presence of
25   BIGOE HENZELL,
           Clerk to Henry Rooke, Esqr.
       JOHN SMALLEY.

AND BE IT REMEMBERED, that the Fifteenth day of July, in the year of our Lord One thousand seven hundred and sixty-nine, the aforesaid
30 Richard Arkwright came before our said Lord the King in His Chancery, and acknowledged the Instrument aforesaid, and all and every thing therein contained and specified, in form above written. And also the Instrument aforesaid was stamp according to the tenor of the Statute made in the sixth year of the reign of the late King and Queen William and Mary of England,
35 and so forth.

Inrolled the Fifteenth day of July, in the year last above written.

Articles of Agreement, 19th June 1769, preserved at the North Western Museum of Science and Industry, Manchester.

terms of the partnership were altered in a document dated 19th June 1769, drawn up between the same three partners, so there may have been a delay while they raised more money. At the time of signing the second agreement, all the partners had moved to Nottingham.

Although it is reported that Arkwright set up a spinning machine in a room adjoining the free grammar school in Preston, there is no record of him ever establishing a commercial enterprise there. For some reason he moved to Nottingham, probably in 1768. Early in March 1768 there were riots and disturbances at Blackburn when the mobs broke up some of Hargreaves' spinning jennies and Hargreaves himself may have been in danger. Hargreaves left Lancashire secretly and moved to Nottingham, and Arkwright probably decided to leave Preston before the same fate overtook him.

While he was trading as an itinerant hair dealer at Wirksworth before 1768, Arkwright had possibly visited Nottingham and made contacts there. It is also suggested that Nottingham, then the centre of an expanding hosiery industry based on the recent inventions of Jedediah Strutt and others, was far more receptive to new inventions and was facing a crisis because the Tewkesbury hosiers were under-selling them. In addition, the type of yarn spun on Arkwright's frame was smoother and harder than that produced on the jenny and was more suited for the hosiery industry.

The three partners rented a site in Nottingham by Goosegate and Hockley for fifty pounds a year, including outhouses, buildings, maltrooms, barn, stableyard, gardens and paddock. Unfortunately the date of this transaction is not given in the documents. The partners must have soon run into financial difficulties because they had to enlarge the partnership in June 1770 by including Samuel Need and Jedediah Strutt.

Ichabod Wright or his son John, the Nottingham bankers, may have introduced Arkwright to these new partners. Arkwright had probably borrowed money from the Wrights, but they must have felt that they could not continue to support technological development on the basis of a long term credit. Both Need and Strutt had long had connections and experience with the textile industry. Need was probably the wealthiest hosier in Nottingham, while Strutt had established a flourishing hosiery business centred on Derby through his patent of 1759 for knitting ribbed stockings. Together they brought enough money into the spinning project to see it through to a successful conclusion. Soon after the partnership was enlarged David Thornley died, and this is the reason why his name has never appeared before in history books.

Very little is known about the early days of this mill at Nottingham, except that it was driven by horses as had been envisaged in the patent. We do not know whether it concentrated solely on spinning cotton or whether it prepared other types of yarn as well. Mills for twisting threads similar to the silk-throwing mills but with long narrow machines had been established in the Nottingham and Birmingham districts many years before this. The trials of the new spinning frame must have proved sufficiently promising for the partners to take the momentous decision to build a mill powered by a waterwheel and to agree to lease a site at Cromford near Matlock from 1st August 1771. From this mill at Cromford, Arkwright's machine received its common name, the waterframe, because it was powered by water. The term water twist denoting a hard smooth yarn survived for many years afterwards even when most mills were driven by steam engines.

Many people have wondered why the partners should have chosen the Cromford site, which was to prove inadequate within a very few years. We know

Opposite The main entrance to the Cromford mills, with the water bridge in the background.

Opposite The Greyhound Hotel at Cromford, built by Arkwright.

from Arkwright's later correspondence with Boulton and Watt about a steam engine that in 1790 the rebuilt mill at Nottingham was driven by six to nine horses, but twenty years earlier it is reasonable to assume it would have been driven by fewer, perhaps only three or four. Therefore it would have been a great step forward to seek a site where a waterwheel of even ten horsepower could be installed.

The site they leased included the river or stream called the Bonsall Brook as well as the Cromford Sough, which drained some lead mines. The sough had a steady flow of water all the year round and was reputed never to freeze, another advantage of the site. Although Cromford was fairly remote, there was a labour force ready to hand in the wives and children of the lead miners living in the district. But the most likely reason for the choice of Cromford may have been that there were no other waterpower sites on the market at that time.

North Street, Cromford. The cottages, and the chapel at the end of the street, were built by Arkwright for his workers.

The remoteness of Cromford may have been one of its advantages because many experiments still had to be made before the venture proved successful. Either to hide their real intentions or because they were still uncertain about the cotton spinning, the land at Cromford was leased "with full liberty and Power and Authority . . . to erect and build one or more Mill or Mills for Spinning Winding or Throwing Silk, Worsted, Linen, Cotton or other materials." They could erect "Waterwheels, Warehouses, Shops, Smithies and other Buildings, Banks, and Dams, Gouts, Shúttles and other conveniencies as they should think proper."* In addition to his mill, Arkwright built rows of cottages for his work people. Some of these had three storeys where looms could be set up on the top floor. He also provided the Greyhound Hotel and a chapel, thus creating the first industrial village, which served as a model for many others.

Early pictures of the mill building show it had five floors well lit by windows along its length.

*Assignment of Mr Smalley's share of the Patent, 1st October 1777, preserved at the N.W.M. of S. & I., Manchester.

Structurally it was similar to the silk-throwing mills built at Derby. Strutt knew Derby well and may have suggested this design for their new mill. Part of the original building still survives (1973) and is used by a firm manufacturing colour pigments. The two top floors have been removed so all that remains now is the stone-built lower part. Building must have started almost as soon as the lease was signed, for in the *Derby Mercury* of 13th December 1771 there appeared the earliest contemporary reference to the mill. The partners were advertising for workmen so the building must have been nearly finished.

**Cotton Mill, Cromford,
10th December 1771.**

WANTED immediately, two Journeymen Clock-makers, or others that understands Tooth and Pinion well: Also a Smith that can forge and file— Likewise two Wood Turners that has been accustomed to Wheelmaking, Spole-turning etc. Weavers residing at the Mill may have good Work. There is Employment at the above Place for Women, Children, etc. and good Wages.

N.B. A Quantity of Box Wood is wanted: Any Persons whom the above may suit, will be treated with by Messrs Arkwright and Co at the Mill or Mr Strutt in Derby.

The clockmakers were very important people in these early cotton mills because all the machinery had to be constructed on site and they were needed to cut and file the teeth on the gearwheels which drove the vital drawing rollers on the waterframes. The women and children were employed on the waterframes while the weavers may have been housed in the cottages to work up the spun cotton.

The only surviving letter of Arkwright's from this vital period was written at Cromford on 2nd March 1772. He wrote to Strutt asking him to see a Mr Ward for some fittings to finish the building, including "those other Locks and also Some sorts of Hangers for the sashes he and you may think best and some good Latches and Catches for the out doors and a few for the inner ones also and a Large Knocker or a Bell to First door." This letter shows that at last Arkwright was satisfied with the performance of his waterframes.

"I have sent a little cotton spun on the one spindle and find no Difficanty in Geting it from the Bobin & Dubeld & Twistd in the maner you see it at one opration. One hand I think will do 40 or 50 lb of it in one day from the bobins it is spun upon, that is in the new whay. I am sertain of it ansuaring & one person will spin a Thousand Hanks a Day so that wee shall not want 1/5 of the hands I First Expected notwithstanding the Roaveing takeing so few. I see Greate Improvements Every day. When I rote to you last had not thorowly provd the spining; several things apening I could not acount for sinse then has proved it."*

Of course alterations were continually being made to improve the efficiency, but it seemed that the immediate problems with the waterframe had been solved satisfactorily. By 1775, the bobbins were automatically raised and lowered so they were filled evenly. This simple improvement must have saved an immense amount of time and cut down the number of people needed to attend the machines, and by 1790 each waterframe had twenty-four spindles on either side, making forty-eight in all.

The letter shows that Arkwright had been spinning and doubling a thread suitable for velvets, but the weaving was not lucrative for "the profits of which

Above Diagram of Arkwright's water frame.
Opposite A water frame built from the diagram. The weights have been detached and put on the floor. The machine's driving drum is on the left.

*R. Arkwright, Letter, 2nd March 1772, preserved at Birmingham Public Library.

will Scairsly pay wharehouse room.'' He also asked
Strutt to try some yarn in a "ribd fraim,'' for he was
certain he could spin yarn for stockings. They were
also experimenting with specially shaped rollers to
spin wool for worsted. Arkwright said he had found a
satisfactory method, but it was other people, who
were unconnected with the Strutts and the Arkwrights, who succeeded in spinning sheep's wool.
Now that they were producing cotton yarn the
partners were faced with two problems, how to sell
it and how to prepare enough roving to supply the
waterframes working continuously.

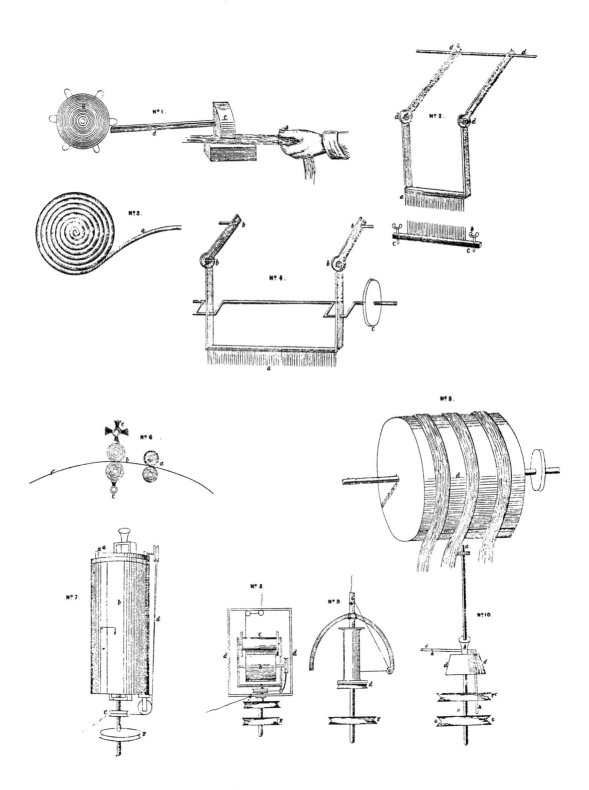

44

3 *The Second Patent*

Having succeeded in producing satisfactory yarn on his waterframe, Arkwright met an unexpected setback to his increasing expansion through the operation of the earlier Calico Acts. The Lancashire industry had obtained partial exemption from both the double duty and the total prohibition on various types of cotton cloth because linen warps were used. Even so their cloth was subject to two excise duties of $1\frac{1}{2}$d., totalling 3d. a yard. The stronger yarn spun on the waterframe enabled weavers to produce cloth made wholly from cotton. In Lancashire, this was accepted by the excise men and charged as printed calico at 3d. a yard, but in London, the excise men considered it must bear the full duty of 6d. a yard.

This anomaly had to be resolved to enable Strutt and Arkwright to continue trading. Accordingly on 25th February 1774, Arkwright petitioned Parliament, pointing out that his machine was "peculiarly adapted for spinning Cotton Yarn for Warps, and is principally used for that Purpose" and that new varieties of velverets and other goods, "particularly a new Manufacture of White Cotton Stuffs adapted for Printing," had been developed, all of which were made entirely in Great Britain.

In London, where the excise officers had decided that the calicos must pay the higher duties of 6d. a yard, many orders received from linen drapers were cancelled "to the great Prejudice of a new and promising *British* manufacture and to the Poor of this Kingdom as well as of the Petitioners."

Prophetically Arkwright saw that

Arkwright's patent specifications for modifications to his spinning machine, dated 1775.

"the said Manufacture, if not crushed by so heavier a Duty as Six Pence a Yard, will rapidly increase, and find new and effectual Employment for many Thousand *British* Poor, and increase the Revenue of this Kingdom . . . and that it is probable that . . . cotton goods so made . . . will be greatly superior in Quality to the present Species of Cotton Goods made with Linen Yarn Warps, and will bleach, print, wash and wear better, and by Means thereof, find further Employment for the Poor."*

Therefore he asked that such goods manufactured wholly in Great Britain should bear only the lower duties and, if exported, should be eligible to the same drawbacks as linen cloth.

The petition was allowed to lie on the table until May when Strutt had to come up to London to help see it through Parliament and also act as a witness. He brought with him various samples of cotton cloth which had been manufactured near Blackburn. In one of his examinations, he claimed that they

"had expended upwards of £13,000 in the said Manufacture; that if charged with the said Duty of Sixpence per Yard, it would totally hinder the Growth, and obstruct the Sale of this promising Manufacture, which, in all Probability, will become a flourishing Trade, if encouraged, and be the Means of employing many Thousands of Poor People there being already upwards of 600 Persons of all Ages employed in this Branch of Business; that Children of Seven Years old, and upwards, are employed, and they prefer Children from Ten to Twelve Years old, for preparing and spinning Cotton by the Said Machine."†

Mr Stephen Williams, a linen draper, said that he had printed between fifty and sixty lengths of this cotton cloth and would have ordered three hundred more but had cancelled his order when the heavier duty was imposed.

Leave was given to bring in a Bill which passed through Parliament without opposition. It was supported by John Plumtree, one of the Nottingham members, and Lord Howe who had close political

House of Commons Journal, vol 34, p. 496, 25th February 1774.
†*House of Commons Journal*, vol 34, p. 709, 6th May 1774.

connections with the area. It received the royal assent on 14th June and, although the export bounty was not granted, the British-made calicos were to be taxed at the lower rate of 3d. a yard. They were to be distinguished from foreign ones by blue threads running down the selvage and each length was to be stamped with the words "British Manufactory." At last the way was clear for expanding sales at home, but a second problem still had to be solved, that of designing preparatory machinery to supply the waterframes.

For the waterframes to be able to spin a continuous yarn, each spindle had to be supplied with a continuous length of roving which in turn had to be made from a continuous length of carded sliver. In

Headstock of a spinning mule made by Asa Lees in 1910. It shows clearly the complicated mechanisms needed to work the machine automatically.

other words, having mechanized one part of the spinning sequence, it was necessary to mechanize all the other parts to restore the balance. This shows how there was a sudden upsurge, which has been called the Industrial Revolution, during which one invention stimulated another in quick succession. Once the balance of the old domestic industry had been upset, invention followed invention until the whole character of textile production was completely changed.

Arkwright's letter shows that in 1772 he was already building other machines besides the water-frames and winding frames in his mill at Cromford. He wrote to Strutt, "At the mill the whant the Cards putting on Andrew might do that as it requires no great judgement." While this could refer to hand cards, it is much more likely that they were experimenting with carding engines.

Paul and Wyatt had found in the 1740s that it was necessary to mechanize carding to keep their spinning machines supplied, but they did not really progress beyond an enlarged hand or stock card. A more significant advance was made by Bourn in 1748 when he patented a carding machine on which the fibres were passed from one cylinder to another. The surfaces of the cylinders were covered with card clothing and the intention was to disentangle the fibres as they passed over three or four cylinders. However, while it was easy to take the fibres off one set of points by another sets of points, Bourn did not solve the problem of taking the fibres off the final set, which had to be done by hand with a needle stick. Here was the real problem of machine carding, which Arkwright eventually solved.

In Lancashire around 1770, the spinning jenny was being continually enlarged, so the problem of carding and supplying rovings was becoming acute there too. Many people tried to make carding engines, as a tombstone in Altham churchyard records:

FORMING LAPS BY HAND.

Above An early hand lap making machine (see p. 50).
Opposite The drawing in the patent specifications of Bourn's carding engine.

"To the memory of John and Ellen Hacking, who invented and made the first carding engine and turned it by hand. They carded cotton wool for their neighbours in Huncoat in the year 1772."*

Soon many horse and waterpowered carding mills were established in Lancashire to provide rovings for the domestic jennies and later the mules. In this county, carding and spinning remained separate for many years. It was Arkwright who united them under one factory roof.

In his patent of 1775, Arkwright claimed that he

"had brought to perfection Certain Instruments or Machines which would be of Public Utility in Preparing Silk, Cotton, Flax and Wool for Spinning and constructed on Principles very different from any that had ever been contrived."†

When the success of his methods of carding and spinning became apparent and people realized the immense fortune he was making, the validity of this second patent was contested and a trial held in 1781. The case went against Arkwright but he succeeded in having the verdict reversed four years later. Then the other cotton spinners, particularly those in Lancashire, went to court again and finally succeeded in having this patent annulled in 1785. The evidence in these trials helps to show what Arkwright was trying to build and also what was being done in other parts of the country.

Descriptions and pictures of ten different machines were given in the patent, but unfortunately they are woefully inadequate and no machine could have been constructed from them. Out of the ten, only five are worth investigating in detail and only one has lasting significance. The originality of all of them has been doubted, but they show the sort of machines Arkwright was building at Cromford and how he was trying to convert the raw cotton into yarn.

The opening and cleaning machines depicted in

*See C. Aspin, *James Hargreaves* (1964), p. 20.

†Patent 1111, 10th April 1775.

the patent were never employed, and there was no
satisfactory machine for doing this until Snodgrass
adapted the threshing machine and produced the
"scutcher" in 1808. About the same time, William
Strutt, son of Jedediah, invented the "devil" at
Belper. The devil began the process of opening and
loosening the cotton which had been tightly com-
pressed into a bale for transhipment. The scutcher
continued this and also cleaned out the seeds and
dirt. At Cromford this must have been done by
women beating the cotton with sticks and picking
out the dirt by hand until it was ready for carding.

The cotton had to be fed into the carding engine.
Arkwright's patent shows he did this by laying a
length of cloth on a table and spreading cotton wool
evenly on top. Then both were rolled up and put at
the back of the carding engine. The fibres were fed
into the points on the carding cylinder as the cloth

A lap making machine: lumps of
cotton are put in the trough on the
left, passed between the left hand
rollers, and wound into a lap
around the small central roller.

CARDING ENGINE
with FLATS

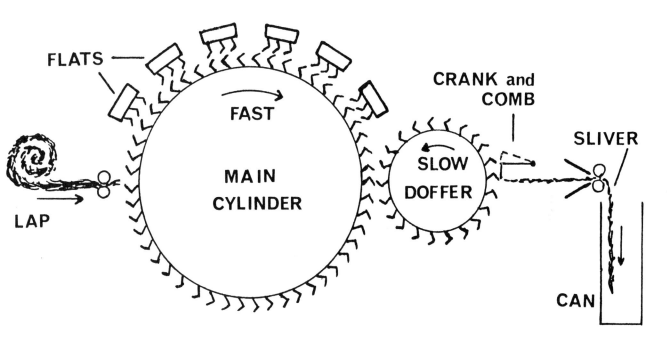

FLATS

FAST

MAIN
CYLINDER

CRANK and
COMB

SLIVER

SLOW
DOFFER

LAP

CAN

was unrolled and fell to the floor. James Lees said at the trial in 1785 that he had found a better method in which a sheet of cloth like a conveyor belt ran on the bottom of a trough and carried forward the cotton which had been piled evenly on top. The cloth returned below the trough in an endless loop. Although Lees' system was better and is still used today in various forms, either method fed the fibres in a steady stream to the carding engine.

On hand cards, the wire hooks were stuck through leather backing about nine inches by six inches in size. To give a continuous sliver from the carding engine, the whole of the surface of the cylinders needed to be covered. With a cylinder about a foot in diameter, which Arkwright used on his first machine, he had to find another method of making the card clothing. So he prepared a long narrow strip which he wound in a spiral round the cylinder so that there were virtually no gaps between the points. In the 1785 trial, Robert Pilkington claimed that he and Richard Livesay had made a carding engine in 1770 with the carding arranged in strips, thus preceding Arkwright.

The type of carding engine which soon became the standard pattern had a main cylinder of large diameter. The cotton was pulled out between the points on the surface of this and much smaller cylinders set round its upper circumference. Later these small cylinders were replaced by flat cards to give a better coverage. A second cylinder, somewhat smaller than the main one, rotated at a different speed to take the carded cotton off, but the problem remained how to take the cotton off this "doffer" cylinder.

In the 1785 trial, a Mr Wood said that at first he had used a fluted roller with needles to strip the cotton off his carding engines but it had damaged the cards. This seems to have been the earliest method tried and it had two other disadvantages: it rubbed the cardings too tightly together so they could not be spun easily, and it only produced short lengths which had to be pieced together (instead of a continuous sliver). Another method used a roller armed with slips of tinplate or iron, which stood erect like the floats of a waterwheel. This, while it may not have damaged the cards so badly, again took the cotton off in short lengths only.

The answer to successful carding was Arkwright's crank and comb, shown in his patent drawing as Figure 4. Across the front of the doffer cylinder was placed a strip of metal, called the comb because the bottom edge was cut into fine teeth. It was connected to a crank which raised and lowered it so that the teeth pushed the cotton off the wire points of the cylinder. The cotton came off in a broad gossamer web which was collected into a single roll, passed through a pair of rollers, and allowed to drop into a

The crank and comb of an early carding machine. The teeth of the comb are hidden by the bar with the bolts on it.

can placed in front. At last a way had been found of taking the carded cotton off in a continuous sliver ready for the next process. The comb survived for nearly two hundred years until the recent development of high-speed carding rendered it obsolete because it was too slow.

At the trial, his widow claimed that James Hargreaves had invented this thirteen or fourteen years earlier, and others claimed they had used it before 1775. But when Arkwright was seeking a retrial, John James, the son of Thomas James who was the partner of Hargreaves, was ready to contradict this evidence and say that Hargreaves obtained the crank and comb surreptitiously from one of Arkwright's workmen.

Another story relates that one of the Lancashire men who worked for Arkwright chalked out the pattern on a table and John James took it to a frame smith to have it made. Soon it was being copied by the machine makers of Nottingham and elsewhere. Therefore it is probable that the crank and comb was invented at Cromford. If so, it is ironical that the only original contribution made by Arkwright or his workmen was taken away from him by law. Although the first carding engines were quite small, it was said that one person using these patent machines could replace nine people using stock cards.

The cotton fibres were caught by the points of the wire hooks on the carding cylinders so most of them were bent when they were pulled off by the comb. For good quality spinning, they needed to be straightened and laid parallel to each other. Even so, however carefully the cotton was fed into the carding engine, there were bound to be irregularities which would appear in the sliver at the other end. In addition, its thick and thin parts caused variations in the final spun yarn. And finally, the sliver was too thick to be fed straight into the waterframes and had to be drawn out thinner before it could be spun.

A later carding machine from Cromford mill. From the lap machine in the background, the lap is placed at the back of the carding engine (on the right), and carded by the rollers and flats as the big main cylinder rotates. The doffer cylinder, crank and comb are on the left.

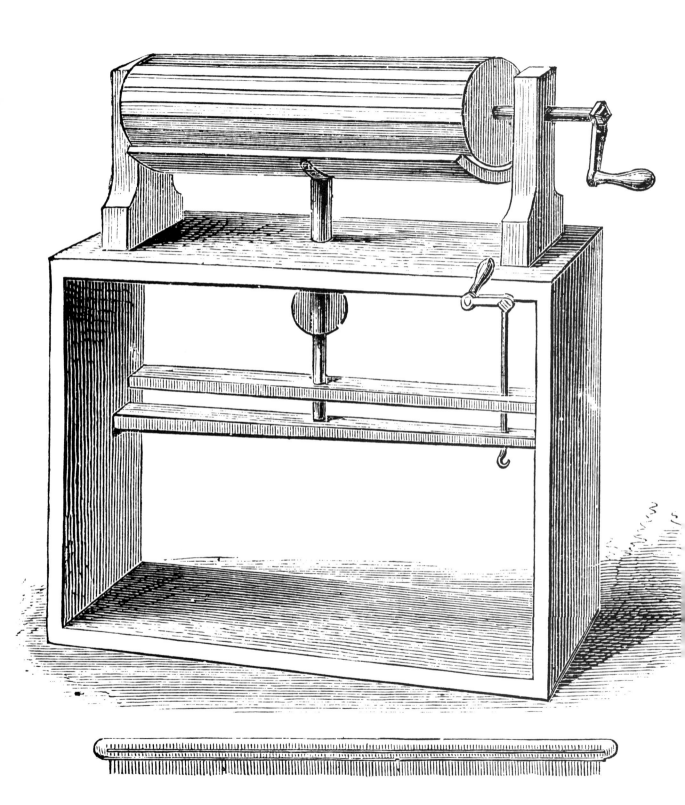

Above A revolving can or lantern frame. The door on the left one is open.
Opposite Paul's cylinder carding machine was patented in 1748 (*see p. 48*). The mechanical removal of the fibres was a tremendous advance.

Therefore Arkwright had to design more machines to overcome these problems and help raise the quality of his final product.

Arkwright was able to solve two of his problems on one machine. By passing the sliver through a set of rollers and drawing it out, he was able to straighten the bent fibres as they were drawn past each other. But the sliver which passed out of the front rollers was too thin and delicate for further handling as it had no twist and Arkwright wanted to draw it out again because he found that the secret of good cotton spinning lay in the drawing. He therefore decided to put four or six slivers through the same rollers and to draw them out in the same ratio as the number he fed in, so he finished with one sliver as thick as each of the originals but four or six times as long. More important, he had a sliver which was much more even because it was unlikely that all the slivers would be thin in the same place and their irregularities balanced each other out.

After passing the slivers through two or even three drawing processes, Arkwright had a good quality sliver, but it was still too thick for his waterframes. He could reduce it by passing it through more rollers, but the thinner sliver had no cohesion and fell to pieces when handled. He realized he must give it enough twist to hold it together in the waterframes, but not too much or it could not be drawn out again. A machine similar to the waterframe could be used to do this but it had to be modified because the slubbing or roving was so very delicate that it could not drag the bobbin round since the friction was enough to break the roving. Arkwright's patent of 1775 shows he tried three different ways to overcome this problem but, although he produced a reasonably satisfactory solution, a more adequate machine was not developed until after his death.

One drawing in the 1775 patent (No. 7) shows the can from a revolving can frame. After passing through rollers and being drawn out, the sliver fell into a tin can. The can in the patent drawing has parallel sides, but later ones were made conical. At the top, the sliver passed through a funnel and then through a pair of rollers (which were later found to be unnecessary) and so into the can. The whole can was rotated so the sliver was twisted as it fell in and was coiled against the side by centrifugal force. When filled, the contents were taken out through a door in the side and carried away to be wound on bobbins ready for the waterframes. Children were employed to do this on winding drums driven either by hand or by power.

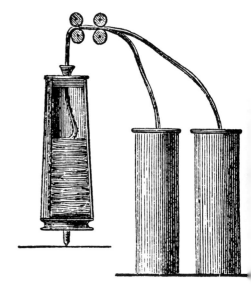

These revolving can frames suffered from many disadvantages but they continued to be employed in mills using the Arkwright system of spinning until the 1830s. It was found that the sliver was not evenly twisted throughout its length and that often the slubbing or roving, as the sliver should be called at this stage, was damaged as the children were winding it onto the bobbins. This extra process of winding was an additional expense which Arkwright himself seems to have recognized. He therefore tried other machines

Drawing No. 8 in the patent shows a device called a "Jack in a Box" which could both twist the sliver and wind it onto the bobbin at the same time. The bobbin rested horizontally on a driving roller so that, as it was filled and the diameter increased, its speed at the circumference remained the same. Both the bobbin and the driving roller were mounted in a frame which was rotated to put in the twist. Arkwright may have found that, as he had to drive the bobbin through the layers of delicate rovings, the rubbing damaged them.

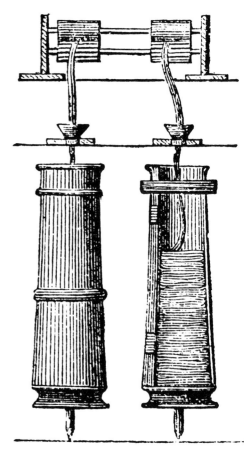

His third picture (No. 9) shows a machine using the same principles as the waterframe, which was later developed successfully into the roving or jack frame, and which has continued to be used until the recent introduction of break spinning. The

Above Arkwright's lantern frame, a modification of the design opposite. *Opposite top and bottom* Front and side view of the machine Arkwright designed for roving cotton.

sliver was drawn out through a set of rollers and a flyer put in the twist before it was wound onto a bobbin. Because the slight friction of the bobbin caused the roving to break, the bobbin was driven by a pulley and band. But here the difficulties started, for the roving had to be wound onto the bobbin at the same speed all the time even though the diameter, and hence the circumference, was increasing as it was filled. As the rollers paid out at the same speed all the time, the speed of the bobbin, but not the flyer, had to decrease in the same ratio as the increasing diameter, or the rovings would be drawn out thinner as the bobbin was filled.

The patent drawing has a sketch of a cone pulley on which a driving band could be moved gradually from the greater to the lesser diameter, but if Arkwright's machine consisted solely of this, it would have been too crude to do the job properly. This type of roving frame, when it was perfected around 1800, had gear drives to the bobbins and spindles so there could be no slipping, and double cone pulleys and other features which would have given much closer speed control

In 1775, Arkwright's second patent shows that he had evolved a series of machines which could be used in conjunction with each other to spin a satisfactory cotton yarn. Of course, since then there have been many improvements, but to Arkwright must go the credit of having established the first production line of machinery which was capable of taking the raw material and converting it into a finished article. It was assisted by human beings only in the processes carrying the product of one machine to the intake of the next and repairing broken threads when necessary. Even though he may have used other people's ideas and advice, it was Arkwright's own perseverance which achieved success at Cromford.

4 *The Exploitation of the Patents*

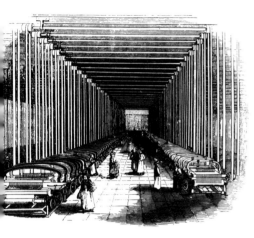

Above The mills needed to cope with the boom in the cotton industry were enormous. The new mill built at Cromford in 1776 was 125 feet long and seven storeys high. This shows another factory where weaving is being carried out. *Opposite* An artist's impression of James Watt experimenting with steam power. *Overleaf* Women workers in cotton mills, *right* in the mid-nineteenth century and *left* in 1920. These women, who are weaving, show the kind of workers who have been vital to the development of the industry.

It is obvious from the text of the 1775 patent that Arkwright and his partners had developed a satisfactory system for spinning cotton by power-driven machinery. Richard Guest, who was antagonistic towards Arkwright, suggested that even as late as 1779 some people thought the undertaking was still hazardous. He even suggested that Arkwright and his wife separated because she was not willing to sell some property which he wished to invest in a cotton spinning venture. But the expansion by 1779 showed that this type of spinning was proving very profitable and that the partners were exploiting their patents to compensate themselves for the risks they had taken.

There were three stages in this exploitation. First there was a period of consolidation in the mill at Cromford, to iron out any technical difficulties and to build up capital. In stage two, the partners themselves built more mills scattered throughout the country. Then their success encouraged other people to take out licences to build mills or to pirate the inventions and build mills in which they clandestinely used the roller drawing system. In this third stage, Arkwright tried to defend his patent rights, but he was finally defeated.

At Cromford, Arkwright soon found himself facing another unexpected difficulty, for he was running short of water to power his mill. There were two reasons for this. When he first moved to Cromford, probably only the waterframes and some winding frames were power-driven, but, as one after another of the preparatory stages was mechanized, so hand processes were replaced by processes needing power. Then, too, there are signs that this mill was enlarged at some stage and again more power would have been required.

He demolished an old corn mill and probably raised the level of the pond supplying his mill, and in this way created a higher fall of water to drive his wheel. At the same time he diverted the course of the Cromford Sough to run in a new channel about two hundred yards from the old one and raised its level with floodgates, either to divert the water into the recently raised mill pond or to drive a second waterwheel. This resulted in raising the water level in the lead mines after it had rained, so the miners retaliated by demolishing the sluice gates. The proprietors of the sough took up the leadminers' cause and the dispute dragged on until 1785, when it was finally agreed that Arkwright was to pay £300 to the proprietors for expenses incurred and repairs to the sough, and in addition he was to pay an annual rent of £20 for the privilege of raising the water for his cotton mills.

In the meantime, Arkwright investigated the possibility of using steam power. In November 1777, he wrote to James Watt who had recently built his first successful steam engines, and three years later he wrote to Watt again. Watt's comments to Matthew Boulton are interesting for the light they throw on Arkwright's character.

"Mr Arkwright of Cromford sent for me last night, he has built a mill and the miners have lett down his water so that it can not move. He is much more modest than he was the last time but dispises your India Reels [for winding silk], he says he can make a thing for that purpose to answer as well for a shilling a piece—but he does not pretend to improving the fire engine now I had little to say against him."*

At this time the steam engine could only pump water, so if Arkwright did install one of eight horsepower, it would have been used to lift the water back up to the

*See R. S. Fitton and A. P. Wadsworth, *The Strutts and the Arkwrights* (1958), p. 80, Watt to Boulton, 12th October 1780.

mill pond after it had flowed past the waterwheel ready for use again. This engine has not been traced, but one may have been installed by some other manufacturer.

During the later part of 1776, Arkwright built a second larger mill at Cromford. The new mill was one hundred and twenty feet long with seven storeys and survived until it was destroyed by fire in 1890. Towards the end of 1776, Arkwright was employing 500 work people at Cromford and after extensions this number rose to 800 in 1789.

It must have become apparent that the site could not be developed any further. Arkwright's son complained to the sough owners in 1821 that the volume of water flowing out of the sough had been seriously diminished by the cutting of a branch level to drain Godber's vein, and as the lead veins were gradually worked out so the volume of water continued to decrease. Cotton spinning became increasingly uneconomic and finally ceased at Cromford in 1846. Yet in the first few years, this venture must have been very profitable, for in 1776 Arkwright was able to set himself up with a carriage.

We do not know how the Cromford mills were financed, but in the next stage of expansion, the partners were responsible for building their own mills, with one exception. This was the mill started in 1777 at Birkacre near Chorley in Lancashire. This was the only mill after the experiments at Nottingham and Cromford to have been financed by the surviving members of the partnership, Arkwright, Strutt, Need, Thomas Walshman and John Cross. This proved to be a short-lived venture, for a period of bad trade followed in 1779 and the textile workers in various parts of Lancashire rioted and smashed up the larger jennies wherever they found them and also attacked ten mills of which Birkacre was the largest.

After being under threat for several days, the mill was attacked and the assailants repulsed; one or two were shot dead. Then the mob returned with firearms and were joined by the Duke of Bridge-water's colliers who helped in a second attack and succeeded in burning the mill down on 4th October. Troops were called in but by then it was too late to save the mill. Serious anxiety was felt throughout the country and Arkwright laid in a supply of arms at Cromford to defend the mills. Besides fifteen hundred small arms, he had "a great Battery of Cannon raised on 9 and 12 Pounders, with great plenty of Powder and Grape Shot, beside which upwards of 500 Spears are fixt in Poles of between 2 and 3 Yards long."* Cromford was never attacked but Birkacre was never rebuilt and the lease was surrendered in 1780.

At this point it is fitting to conclude the story of the other joint venture, the Nottingham mill. This was developed into quite a substantial four storey building and was employing 300 people by 1772. In November 1781 it was destroyed by a fire which

"raged with such Fury, that in two Hours after the spacious Building was reduced to a mere Shell. All the Machines, Wheels, Spindles, etc employed for spinning and winding Cotton were entirely consumed, and not a single Article contained therein, (the Books Excepted) could possibly be saved, notwithstanding the Exertions of many Inhabitants, who used their utmost to preserve it and the adjacent House, from Inevitable Destruction. From what cause the Fire originated, we are not able to tell."†

It was soon rebuilt under the title of Arkwright & Co., and was still driven by horsepower. In 1790, Arkwright decided to install a steam engine and approached Boulton and Watt for their advice. The horsewheel was twenty-seven feet in diameter and was driven by six to nine horses which seem to have been overworked, for the main shaft was turning too slowly. Therefore it was decided to erect a twelve horse rotative engine, but it is not known how long the mill continued working afterwards.

*Fitton and Wadsworth, *op. cit.*, p. 79.

†*Derby Mercury*, 15th November 1781.

Except for the Birkacre mill, Samuel Need played no further part in the expansion. Probably the partnership between Arkwright and Strutt was terminated on Need's death. Earlier in 1777, Arkwright had picked a quarrel with John Smalley and turned him out of the partnership. This dispute will be mentioned later when Arkwright's character is being discussed.

Smalley was paid over £3,200 by the remaining partners and retired to Holywell in Flintshire. As part of the settlement, he may have been given a licence for building waterframes, which, together with the money, enabled him to build a three storey mill. He died at Holywell in 1782, but his sons continued cotton spinning and built two larger mills there in 1783 and 1785. Textile production continues at this site right up to the present day (1973).

Jedediah Strutt purchased land at Belper, a little further downstream from Cromford on the Derwent towards Derby. Here he tamed the vicious floods of that river by building a large semi-circular weir and damming the water up in a vast lake over 22 acres in extent. One mill was working by 1778 and others were added in 1786 and 1793. With various additions and rebuildings, this was to become one of the largest cotton-spinning sites in the country and the water has been used to drive the mills right up to the present day.

Nearly two miles downstream at Milford, Strutt purchased a second site in 1777. Here two mills had been established before 1800 and in 1792 the famous warehouse was begun in which the Strutts experimented with a fireproof structure. This has now been demolished. In 1815, all these mills were employing 1,494 people, a little fewer than the 1,600 claimed by Robert Owen at New Lanark.

Strutt concentrated his developments at these two sites, but Arkwright, either by himself or in partnership with local people, began to establish mills scattered throughout the country. His first seems to have been Lumford Mill at Bakewell, not far from Cromford. Here again he ran into trouble with his water supplies, for he diverted the river Wye from its ancient course to the Duke of Rutland's corn mill, cut through the mill dam, and took soil, gravel and stone from waste ground belonging to the Duke in order to construct dams and ponds. The dispute with the Duke was settled in 1786 by which time Arkwright had handed over the running of the mill to his son.

On the river Derwent and its tributaries, Arkwright was also associated with mills at Cressbrook (1779), Wirksworth (1780), and Masson (1783). Cressbrook was a short-lived venture in its original building for

The large, water-powered cotton mill built by Strutt at Belper, Derbyshire, in the 1770s.

it was burnt down in November 1785; the *Derby Mercury* reported that two small boys who had come to watch the fire were drowned in the mill pond. It does not seem to have been rebuilt until 1815, which is surprising. Masson mill has been more fortunate for the impressive building of 1783 still remains in use for textiles. It was built close to an existing paper mill on the river Derwent and the arch-shaped weir and water-courses can be seen as well as the ornate entrance of the original building.

Further afield, Arkwright purchased Tutbury mill at Rocester in 1781 for £820 and rebuilt it. This is another mill still used for textiles and the old part of it can be easily distinguished. A mill at Keighly in the West Riding of Yorkshire is said to have begun spinning in 1780 and another in the same year at Ashbourne in Derbyshire. In 1783 mills were opened at Bromsgrove in Worcestershire and on Shudehill, Manchester. Arkwright started this latter mill in partnership with two local men, but handed over his share to his son soon afterwards. As the stream was not big enough to drive it, and as at this date no successful rotative steam engine had been developed, a steam pumping engine was used to raise the water back to the upper mill pond so it could be used over and over again to drive a waterwheel.

In October 1784, Arkwright visited Scotland and was fêted at Glasgow, given a dinner there and made an honorary burgess and guild brother. He was also given the freedom of the city of Perth. During his visit, David Dale, one of the important Glasgow cotton merchants, took him to Lanark to see the Falls of Clyde. Arkwright realized their great potential as a source of power and helped Dale build the first of the New Lanark mills which was begun in April 1785 and was spinning by March 1786. The partnership did not last long; one account says it finally broke up over a dispute about the siting of the

Opposite The first mill built by Robert Owen at New Lanark in 1785. Originally it was two storeys higher.
Below Haarlem mill, Wirksworth. As the stream proved too small to drive the mill, Arkwright installed a steam engine in 1780.

mill bell. Dale won and the bell still hangs on top of a block of flats opposite the mill entrance. The river here could produce on average 650 horsepower and continued to be used until the mills closed around 1969. This was the famous site where Robert Owen conducted his social experiments.

Seeing the success of Arkwright's mills, other people wanted to try their luck too. Unfortunately very little is known about the licences which the partners sold to allow other people to build their machines. It seems that licences were sold for units of one thousand spindles, which, judging by later calculations, would have needed ten horsepower to drive them. Gardom and Pares, the partnership which built the mill at Calver on the Derwent around 1780, paid £2,000 for using the first patent, £5,000 for using the second and an annual payment of £1,000. Ironically one of the first licensees was James Hargreaves who, shortly before his death, was forced to sell the jennies in his Nottingham mill, and, with the help of his partner Thomas James, had to re-equip with waterframes.

In Lancashire, Messrs Collinson and Watson had started a mill at Preston, and Robert Peel had an early mill either at Bury or at Burton on Trent. Possibly he started with jennies in one and water-frames in the second. Arkwright said he sold licences to numbers of adventurers in the Midlands as well as elsewhere. What happened to these payments after Need's death in 1781 is not known. What is known is that people felt that Arkwright charged excessively and this encouraged them to build his machines without seeking permission.

While it is difficult to find out who was using Arkwright's patents legally, it is impossible to discover how many people were infringing them. John Lees at Oldham was reputed to have been the first person in that area to use waterframes but he never paid any royalties. In 1781 Gardom and Pares, and

The bell turret on top of the workers' flats built by Owen at New Lanark.

possibly others, stopped paying royalties partly because they felt they had paid more than enough and partly because others were using the patents freely.

Arkwright decided to take steps to protect himself. He approached three spinners, John Middleton of Tideswell, Henry Marsland of Bullock Smithy near Stockport, and Daniel Lees of Oldham, who had infringed his carding patent. They submitted and paid up, but when he decided to take nine more to trial, he found that the Lancashire manufacturers had had time to organize resistance. The first case to be heard at the Court of King's Bench was against Colonel Mordaunt who had a small mill with six hundred spindles at Halsall near Ormskirk. Arkwright lost the case in June 1781, and so his second patent became void.

His first patent still ran until July 1783, but Arkwright wished to secure greater profits for himself. In 1775, James Watt had managed to persuade Parliament to prolong his patent until 1800, so in 1782 Arkwright petitioned Parliament to extend his first patent until 1789 when the second would have expired and to confirm the second.

He claimed that "many Years intense Study and painful Application, and after a great Variety of repeated experiments" were needed to invent his machine. He had "expended considerable Sums of Money" before he obtained his patent in 1769 and then "after several Years further Study and Assiduity . . . and after a large additional Expense incurred therein brought the same to a greater Degree of Perfection." He claimed that "For near Five years after the obtaining of the First Patent in the year 1769, though more than Twelve thousand Pounds had been expended, so far from any Profit accruing to Mr *Arkwright* and his Partners, they were the losers of above *Five hundred Pounds.*"*

Together with the experiments for his second patent,

*A State of the Facts Respecting the Case of Mr Richard Arkwright (1783).

Swanson and Burley's cotton factory near Preston, Lancashire. *Overleaf* Interior of a cotton mill. On the left are the great machines to card the fibres.

he and his partners had expended the sum of £30,000 and upwards and also had lost four or five thousand pounds by "the Violence of riotous and ill disposed Persons, who have burnt and destroyed his Buildings . . ."* at Birkacre.

The opposition from Lancashire proved too strong and his petition was rejected, largely because he had charged too much for his patents and had made a large enough fortune already. As the merchants and traders of Liverpool said, he had "realized such a Fortune as every unprejudiced Person must allow to be an ample compensation for the most happy Efforts of Genius."†

Arkwright tried again in 1783 to persuade Parliament to prolong his patent but again he was defeated. Therefore many people began to build cotton-spinning mills because the roller spinning patent expired that year. Such was the rush to build mills that early in 1785 it was reckoned that £150,000 had been spent.

Most people would not have attempted to turn this tide, but Arkwright was determined not to give in so easily. In February that year, he sued a

**House of Commons Journal*, vol 38, p. 687, 6th February 1782.
†Ibid, vol 38, p. 687, 6th February 1782.

near neighbour, Peter Nightingale, for infringing his second patent. Nightingale, a lead merchant, had branched out into cotton spinning the year before when he built his Lea Mill, and so he had not infringed the earlier patent. The case was fought out in the Court of Common Pleas where James Watt gave evidence on behalf of Arkwright. It was suspected that there was some collusion for Nightingale's defence was badly organized and Arkwright won.

This threw the whole of the Lancashire trade into confusion, but they managed to have the case reopened and brought a formidable array of witnesses against Arkwright. Amongst them were Thomas Highs and John Kay, who for the first time claimed the credit for the roller spinning invention. Evidence from this trial has been quoted in chapter 3 to explain the 1775 patent so it will not be examined again. There is no doubt that, if he had won, Arkwright would have had the whole of the cotton trade at his mercy because the crank and comb provided the best way of stripping the doffer cylinders on carding engines.

By this time Crompton's mule was gaining in popularity so there were three different spinning machines but no other way of carding. Some of the evidence is now doubted, but the wording in the patent specification was very vague and certainly no machine could have been built from the descriptions and the pictures. Arkwright lost the case in July, but tried to have it reopened in the following November. He was not allowed to do this so the patents were, finally, freely available to all.

Although finer counts of cotton yarn could be spun on Crompton's mule than were possible by hand spinning or the waterframe, in 1785 there were only about 1,000 mule spindles in existence. The early 1790s, however, saw a switch to mule spinning. Waterframes continued to be used in waterpowered mills for spinning for the hosiery trade, sewing thread

and some of the heavier counts. Then soon after 1800 the waterframe was improved into the "throstle" which in its turn was replaced by the ringframe.

Mules are now almost extinct and the ringframe, whose ancestry can be traced back through Arkwright's invention, reigns supreme. Carding until recently has relied exclusively on the crank and comb. Therefore Arkwright's contributions have been vital to the growth of the textile industry, and if he had not tried to exploit his patents so harshly, he might have had them extended. Matthew Boulton summed up the contemporary feeling about him:

"Tyranny and an improper exercise of power will not do in this country. . . . If he [Arkwright] had been a more civilised being and had understood mankind better, he would now have enjoyed his patent."*

*H. W. Dickinson, *Matthew Boulton* (1937), pp. 128–9.

Mule spinning in a cotton mill. Many hundreds of threads could be produced while relatively few people kept an eye on the machines.

5 *A Happy Mechanic*

So far, we have only considered Arkwright's technical achievements, but without a business approach and some qualities of leadership, he could not have made his immense fortune. He did not have an easy relationship with his partners and made enemies, as any successful man will, but he seems to have managed his work people well which may account for his technical success.

Somebody must have been responsible for developing all the complex machinery at Cromford. Thornley through his death and Need, who gave only financial support, may be discounted. There is no tradition that Smalley contributed any mechanical idea although he lived at Cromford and helped to manage the mill. Strutt with his mechanical ability proved by his earlier inventions helped a little, but in the vital year preceding the 1775 patent went to London as a witness for the Calico Act and did not return for a very long time through his wife's death and his own ill health.

From this one is forced to assume that Arkwright must receive the credit for developing the cotton-spinning machinery. His workmen may have suggested some of the ideas, one example being the heart-shaped cam for raising and lowering the bobbins so they were filled evenly, which has sometimes been attributed to Samuel Slater. It still needed someone to realize the potential of these suggestions and see they were put into practice.

If Arkwright were the major designer, then he has never been given the credit he deserves for pioneering the first production line of machines in the world engaged in a manufacturing process. It was no inconsiderable achievement to design, develop

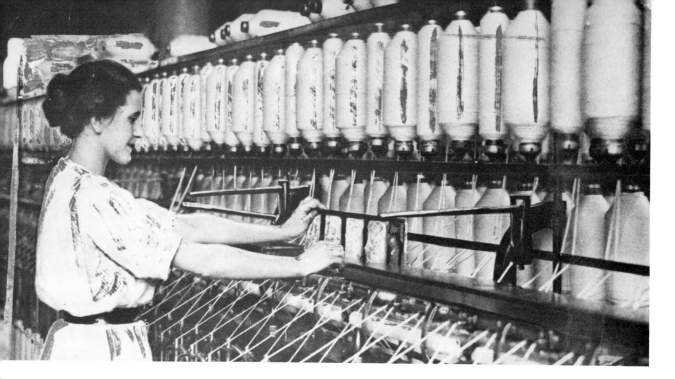

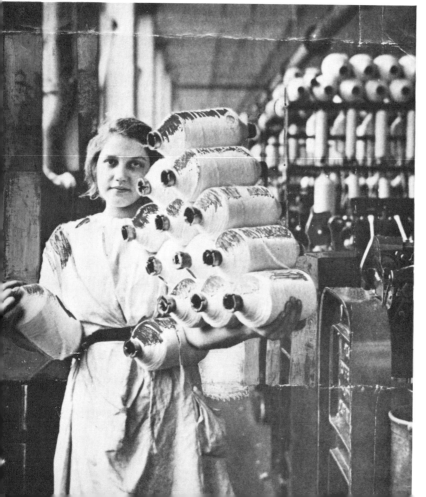

Above The roving frame in a
Lancashire cotton mill, 1919.
Left A girl carries bobbins of cotton
to the roving frame.
Opposite Child labour in a nineteenth
century mill. Thanks to the various
Factory Acts, children were no
longer employed in the mills, and
working hours were not as long as
they had been.

and produce the variety of machines needed to spin cotton mechanically, and he may also have had to create special machine tools for making some of the parts for his textile machines.

In addition Arkwright had to find the labour force to operate his mill. At first he may have been able to find labour locally, but his advertisement in the *Derby Mercury*, December 1771, shows he soon outstripped the local supply (see page 41). Although he did use indentured labour, there is no record that he employed pauper apprentices at Cromford, something which became a grim aspect of many later mills using his machinery. He did of course employ child labour, but as the following advertisement shows, he seems to have preferred bringing large families to Cromford instead of orphans or parish apprentices.

"Wanted at Cromford . . . Forging or Filing Smiths, Joiners and Carpenters, Framework-Knitters and Weavers, with large Families. Likewise Children of all Ages; above seven years old, may have constant Employment. Boys and young Men may have Trades taught them, which will enable them to maintain a Family in a short time."*

Derby Mercury, 20th September 1781.   77

Shift work was practised in most of these early mills and Cromford was no exception, with the machinery running day and night. The famous artist, Wright of Derby, painted Cromford mill at night. To contemporaries, this seemed wonderful, as did the fact that young children could earn their livelihood.

An early visitor to Cromford about 1776, William Bray, remarked that about 200 persons were employed there. They worked in turn both night and day. He saw the second mill and new houses in course of erection and thought "everything wears the face of industry and cheerfulness."* Day and night working at Cromford was confirmed by Archibald Buchanan, the important Scottish spinner, who learnt his trade at Cromford and said, "The spinning went on at night; the preparation was made in the day," suggesting that there was a shortage of power. At this time the shift was generally twelve hours with an hour's break for lunch or dinner.

Once a year in September, Arkwright held a festival for his work people. In 1776 and again two years later this was turned into something of a public spectacle. In the first year he was celebrating the completion of the building of his second mill and about 500 workmen and children, and a boy working a loom, led by a band, paraded round the village, watched by a large crowd. On their return to the mill, they were suitably regaled with ale and buns and a ball followed in the evening. In 1778, a song praising Arkwright was composed and sung at the festival, and again a ball was given in the evening.

Three years later in 1781, a visiting doctor, Sylas Neville, noted that Arkwright

"by his conduct appears to be a man of great understanding & to know the way of making his people do their best. He not only distributes pecuniary rewards, but gives distinguishing dresses to the most deserving of both sexes, which excites great emulation. He also gives two Balls at the Greyhound

*Fitton & Wadsworth, *op. cit.,* p. 98.

to the workmen & their wives & families with a weeks jubilee at the time of each ball. This makes them industrious and sober all the rest of the year."*

There is also a record of Arkwright giving twenty-seven fine milch cows to his principal workmen in 1783 and then in 1790 he was able to get a market established in Cromford. Here again he provided prizes for the best stallholders. The market must have helped solve the problem of provisioning his working force for Cromford was still very remote. He also sponsored sick clubs and provident societies and by 1790 there were no less than eight in and about Cromford.

In these ways, Arkwright kept his labour force happy. In contrast with this, his relations with his partners seem to have been constantly difficult. There was friction between Smalley and Arkwright in 1773. Strutt tried to calm things down and wrote out the draft of a letter to Smalley on the back of one he had received from his wife:

> "Am sorry to find matters betwixt you & Mr Arkwright are come to such extremities (*it is directly contrary to my disposition*) & wonder he shoud persist in giving you fresh provocations. I said what I coud to persuade him to oblige you in anything that was reasonable & to endeavour to live on good terms at least & my Wife has said a great deal to him (*and what I can do more I cannot stop his mouth nor is it in my power to convince him*) nor when I come to consider the matter seriously and the circumstances I am at a loss to think about what we can do it, you must be sensible when some sort of people set themselves to be perverse it is very difficult to prevent them being so. We can not (*stop his mouth or prevent his doing wrong*) prevent his saying Ill natured things nor can we regulate his actions . . ."† [parts in italics crossed out in original.]

Trouble flared up again in February 1777 when Strutt once more tried to make peace and wrote to Smalley:

> "Mr Arkwright has been here today to acquaint me, and is now gone to Nottm. to acquaint Mr Need of his absolute determination of a Seperation betwixt him and you . . . If you would agree to separate from Mr Arkwright he has proposed

*Cozens-Hardy (ed.), *The Diary of Sylas Neville, 1767–1788* (1950), p. 279.

†Fitton & Wadsworth, *op. cit.*, p. 75.

to leave the conditions to such indifferent persons as he and you shall make choice of . . . [Consider] whether this compensation before a break has taken place will not be more than you or any of us shall receive when there is an open rupture & a Law suit commenc'd & a business carried on in opposition to this; all which I believe will be the case if not prevented—I wish you seriously to consider these circumstances in that point of view that immediately affects your own interest & without mentioning how much I & Mr Need shall be injured who should have no concern in this quarrel."*

Smalley agreed to these proposals and suggested a meeting at Matlock Bath on 24th February, and Arkwright put off his threatened trip to London. But the two sides were not reconciled and Smalley received £3,202 16s 5½d as recompense for his share in the partnership. Arkwright had threatened to

*Letter from Strutt to Smalley, 9th February 1777, preserved at the N.W.M. of S. & I., Manchester.

Above Women at work with power driven weaving looms.
Opposite top A satirical cartoon by Cruikshank to show the plight of the child workers in the textile mills.
Opposite below Mill girls in a Manchester cotton factory, *c.* 1870.

dissolve the partnership, by force if necessary. He again behaved in the same way in 1785 when he was deprived of his patent, for he threatened to publish plates or drawings of his machinery and send them abroad so foreigners could copy them.

After he lost his patent case, Arkwright called a meeting of fellow patentees which agreed to recommend that the detailed specifications necessary with each application for a patent should not be made public, but this came to nothing. Afterwards Wedgwood mentioned to Sir Joseph Banks a plan suggested by Arkwright for a statutory monopoly for spinning wool. Arkwright would adapt his waterframe to spin wool and, in return for an Act of Parliament giving him the sole right, he would "spin wool 50 per cent cheaper than it is now spun, which 50 per cent will be entire gain to the public—and so much cheaper still, that he himself will be content with one half of the surplus profit above the 50 per cent, the other half to belong to the person whom he instructs in the business."*

Nothing came of this idea. The waterframe was adapted to spin worsted but never woollens (see page 31).

The cotton-spinning venture probably began to show profits from some time in 1775. Arkwright himself said that for the first five years of the 1769 patent they had lost money, but in 1776 the partners began to expand at Cromford and their profits probably began to increase rapidly from that point. In July 1775, Arkwright had purchased a very elegant little watch from Manchester for his daughter. A further sign of prosperity appeared a year later when Arkwright set up his own carriage and horses and in that same year he gave his people the festival at Cromford.

By 1780, it could be written:

"With in the small space of ten years, from being a poor man not worth £5, now keeps his carriage and servants, is become a Lord of a Manor, and has purchased an estate of £20,000."†

When he died in 1792, he left, as the *Gentleman's Magazine* put it,

"Manufactures the income of which is greater than that of most German principalities... His real and personal property is estimated at little short of half a million."

Of course not all of this wealth came from his own mills. In the 1780s, Arkwright concentrated more on helping to finance other people's projects. Some of his mill speculations with other partners in both England and Scotland have been mentioned already (see page 62). Then, for some years starting in 1783, he helped to finance Samuel Oldknow, the Stockport

Wedgwood's Common Place Book, p. 325–6 (Etruria Museum).

†R. Mather, *Impartial Representation of the Case of the Poor Cotton Spinners in Lancashire* (1780).

cotton merchant, who employed a great many muslin weavers. This was a good outlet for yarn and the connection was maintained by his son. Another financial venture was a secret loan of £5,000 to Georgina, Duchess of Devonshire, to help pay her gambling debts. In 1788, Arkwright wrote to her about the repayment of this money but she must have defaulted for in 1801 the principal was still owing, although the interest was being paid to Richard Arkwright junior.

Little is known about his other investments. Like others at that time, he gradually purchased a large estate around Cromford, including the Lordship of the Manor which would have been attached to one

Overleaf The fruits of successful invention: Willersley Castle, the house Arkwright built for himself, overlooking the river Derwent. The town centre of Rochdale, its fine buildings and the spacious layout all based on the wealth obtained from the cotton industry. (*Below*)

particular estate. Here, just out of sight of his mills, he decided to build a Gothic style mansion, Willersley Castle. He spent £3,000 clearing away a huge rock and had the gardens landscaped. Unfortunately the house was damaged by fire in 1791 before it was completed. Most of the furniture was saved and his son finished it.

In 1787, Arkwright reached the height of his social ambition when he was made High Sheriff of Derbyshire. He was an Anglican and therefore not barred from such offices as were non-conformists. He performed the office with considerable display, for he had thirty javelin-men dressed in the richest liveries ever seen on such an occasion, while during the assize, he provided a plentiful table with the choicest wines, and his coach was very elegant and fashionable. During his period of office, he was knighted for presenting a loyal address to George III.

Below and overleaf A sudden flowering of invention in the eighteenth century changed the making of textiles from the essentially domestic craft it had been since man first spun and wove, to the vast, factory-based industry it is now, only two hundred years later.

With his knighthood, Arkwright had become socially acceptable. He was respected by his fellow industrialists who followed his example. As Sir Robert Peel put it, "Arkwright originated the buildings; we all looked up to him and imitated his building."* Wedgwood was favourably impressed by him yet Carlyle described him as a "Plain almost gross, bag-cheeked, pot-bellied Lancashire man, with an air of painful reflection, yet also of copious free digestion."

It is interesting that William Nicholson, searching for material to write a biography in 1799, could not decide whether Arkwright was a superior genius and a remarkable inventor, or a cunning schemer and collector of other men's inventions, supporting them by borrowed capital. What he himself invented and what he borrowed from others will never be sorted out now. Even if he did steal his inventions from other people, he showed remarkable skill and organizing ability in creating his spinning empire and deriving such profits from it.

Perhaps the best comments on the significance of Arkwright's achievements are the figures of the amount of cotton imported between 1771 and 1790.†

Although some of this cotton would have been

Year	Lb Cotton Imported
1771–75	4,764,589 average per year
1776–80	6,766,613
1781	5,198,778
1782	11,828,039
1783	9,735,663
1784	11,482,083
1785	18,400,384
1786	19,475,020
1787	23,250,268
1788	20,467,436
1789	32,576,023
1790	31,447,605

*Fitton & Wadsworth, *op. cit.*, p. 98.

†E. Baines, *History of the Cotton Manufacture in Great Britain*, (1835), p. 215.

spun on jennies and towards the end of the period on mules, nearly all of it would have been carded with the crank and comb. It will be remembered that cotton spun on the waterframe was particularly suited for the warp of calico cloth, and indeed that a new industry grew up based on these machines. The excise duties on calico cloth show a remarkable change. At first most of it was imported, but later a much larger amount was produced at home. This gives another indication of the importance of Arkwright's inventions because the yarn from his waterframes replaced linen as the warp for this material.

Yards of Cloth on which Duties were imposed*

Year	British Calicos, Yards	Foreign Calicos, Yards
1775	56,814	2,111,439
1776	103,147	1,783,422
1777	201,253	1,947,570
1778	385,930	1,913,004
1779	656,245	1,342,744
1780	1,143,043	1,071,775
1781	2,318,972	1,194,495
1782	2,635,155	964,897
1783	3,578,590	770,922

After the unrest of 1779, a Committee of Parliament investigated the complaints against Arkwright's patent machines. They found that cotton manufacture in Lancashire had doubled during the previous ten years and that a new calico manufacturing industry had been established which owed its existence to these machines. They also found

"That the Demand for Cotton Goods could not have been supplied if the Machines had not been made use of—That Cotton Goods were never made better than they have been within the last Five Years; and that fewer Complaints of them have been made by their Correspondents abroad

*Fitton & Wadsworth, *op. cit.*, p. 75.

since the Introduction of the Patent Machines than before—
That there are three times as many Looms employed now, as
there were Ten Years ago; and that if there were many more
Looms than there are at present, the Manufacturers would
be glad to employ them—That if the Spinning Machines
were prevented from working, it would not be possible to
supply the weaver with warp equal to the present Demand."*

This quotation shows how important Arkwright's
waterframes had become in the textile industry.
Other industries were affected too. To give one
example, almost two thirds of the rotative steam
engines built by Boulton and Watt were installed in
textile mills. If there had been only the inventions of
Hargreaves and Crompton, the textile industry
might never have developed from the domestic into
a mill-based industry.

This was Arkwright's achievement which formed
one of the foundation stones of the Industrial
Revolution. Edward Baines, writing in 1835, even
thought that the cotton industry had saved England:

"The Cotton Manufacture arose in this country at a critical
period of our history. England had just lost her American
colonies; but that loss was more than compensated by this
new source of prosperity springing up at home. The genius
of our mechanics repaired the errors of our statesmen. In the
long and fearful struggle which followed the French
Revolution this country was mainly supported by its
commerce; and the largest, though the newest branch of that
commerce was furnished by the cotton manufacture. To
Arkwright and Watt, England is far more indebted for her
triumphs than to Nelson and Wellington. Without the
means supplied by her flourishing manufactures and trade,
the country would not have born up under a conflict so
prolonged and exhausting."†

Although the machines used in the textile industry
today are made entirely from metal with streamlined
exteriors and soon few will be left using his roller
drawing or his crank comb, their origins can be
traced directly back to the primitive wooden
machines which Arkwright struggled to build.

Because textiles are a necessity of life, their pro-

*House of Commons Journal, vol 37, 27th June 1780, p. 926.

†Baines, op. cit., p. 503.

duction forms a vital economic and social function in every civilization which is too often taken for granted. Arkwright, and his immediate successors, radically changed the whole aspect of textile production and helped to create the basis for our modern society.

Such are the results of his mechanical ingenuity, but it is far more difficult to give an appraisal of his character. Perhaps this is best left to one of his contemporaries, Samuel Salte:

> "Mr Arkwright was a happy mechanic. In his lifetime he has received the reward of his ingenuity—it does not happen so in general."*

Date Chart

1350	Jersey spinning wheel began to be introduced.
1400	Saxony spinning wheel began to be introduced.
1586	Ribbon loom possibly invented in Dantzig by Anton Moller.
1589	Rev. William Lee invented the knitting machine.
1717	Thomas Lombe established the first successful silk-throwing mill powered by water in this country at Derby.
1732	Richard Arkwright born.
1733	John Kay patented his flying shuttle.
1738–48	Paul and Wyatt experimented with their unsuccessful attempts to build a spinning machine.
1759	Jedediah Strutt patented a method of making ribbed knitting on the knitting machine.
1760	Robert Kay invented the drop box on looms for weaving with three or four different shuttles.

*Oldknow Papers, No. 751, from S. & W. Salte, 5th November 1787 (John Rylands Library, Manchester).

	J. de Vaucanson built a power loom in France but it was too complicated for general use.
1763–5	James Hargreaves made his spinning jenny.
1769	Arkwright patented his roller spinning machine.
1771	Arkwright's waterpowered mill at Cromford was built.
1775	Arkwright patented ways of carding the cotton and preparing it for spinning. The most important of these was the crank and comb.
1779	Samuel Crompton perfected his spinning mule.
1785	Rev. Edmund Cartwright patented his first power loom, but it needed much more development before it could be used commercially.
1792	Arkwright died.

For Further Reading

C. Aspin and S. D. Chapman, *James Hargreaves and the Spinning Jenny* (Helmshore, 1964).

E. Baines, *The Cotton Manufacture in Great Britain* (London, 1835).

S. D. Chapman, *The Early Factory Masters* (Newton Abbot, 1967).

R. S. Fitton and A. P. Wadsworth, *The Strutts and the Arkwrights* (Manchester, 1958).

R. Guest, *A Compendious History of the Cotton-Manufacture, with a Disproval of the Claim of Sir Richard Arkwright to the Invention of its ingenious Machinery* (Manchester, 1823).

R. L. Hills, *Power in the Industrial Revolution* (Manchester, 1970).

Glossary

BREAK SPINNING   This modern method of spinning does not use rollers for drawing out the cotton but a vacuum sucks the fibres through a tube and they are twisted as they emerge at the other end.

CALICO   is a fairly heavy cotton cloth which originated in Egypt.

CARDING   Both wool fibres on the sheep and cotton fibres in a boll are entangled together in their natural state. Disentangling them and beginning to lay them parallel is called carding.

CARD CLOTHING   This is the leather or cloth backing with wires stuck through it to form points. This card clothing is nailed to a piece of wood to form a hand card or wrapped round cylinders on the machines.

COUNTS   The fineness of a cotton yarn is measured in counts. If a cotton yarn is count one, then 840 yards of it will weigh one pound. The count is determined by how many hanks, each 840 yards, weigh one pound.

CRANK AND COMB   In front of the doffer or final cylinder on his carding engine, Arkwright fitted a crank and comb to remove the cotton. The crank, as it rotated, raised and lowered the comb which knocked the cotton off the points of the card clothing on the doffer cylinder.

DEVIL   The devil was the first stage in preparing the cotton for spinning. It was like a carding engine but had iron spikes instead of the card clothing. It broke up the lumps of cotton from the bale.

DOUBLING   Doubling is running two or more yarns together and twisting them so they will not unwind, for example sewing cotton or knitting wool.

DRAFTING OR DRAWING   The process of pulling out the fibres until the sliver or roving is thin enough for spinning.

FLAX WHEEL   see SAXONY WHEEL.

FLYER   The flyer is a horseshoe-shaped piece of wood or metal fitted onto the end of the spindle. It guides the yarn to the side of the bobbin so it can be wound on.

FLYING SHUTTLE   John Kay fitted small wheels to an ordinary shuttle so it could run on a ledge fitted to the reed of a loom. The shuttle was driven from side to side by hammers and so termed the flying shuttle.

GREY CLOTH   This is cloth which has come straight from the loom and still needs cleaning or bleaching and finishing.

JENNY   This was the name commonly given to the spinning machine invented by James Hargreaves between 1763 and 1765.

JERSEY WHEEL   This was the first type of spinning wheel which had only a plain spindle and was always turned by hand. It is sometimes called the great wheel because the flywheel is much larger than on any other type of spinning wheel.

MULE   This was the name commonly given to the spinning machine perfected by Samuel Crompton in 1779. It had rollers for drawing out the cotton but plain spindles like the Jersey wheel and the jenny. The spindles were placed on a moving carriage and it had an intermittent spinning cycle.

MUSLIN   This was a fine type of cotton cloth.

NEEDLE STICK   This was a bar with a row of spikes or needles sticking out along it so the bar can be held in the hand and the needles used to pull off the fibres from a hand card.

OPENING   This is the first process of loosening the tightly packed bales of cotton.

PICKING   This is removing the dirt, seeds and seed pods from the cotton. This was at first done by hand, hence the term.

PIRN   A small bobbin on which the weft is wound so it can be placed in a shuttle.

POINTS   These are the wire hooks which are stuck through leather or cloth backing to make the clothing for hand cards or carding engines.

QUILL   see PIRN.

REED   To make a firm compact cloth on a loom, the weft must be beaten up hard against the preceding shoot or thread. This is done by the reed which is like a comb with its teeth sliding along the warp threads.

ROVING   A fairly thick rope of fibres loosely twisted together so it has enough cohesion to prevent it easily disintegrating but not enough to prevent it being drawn out again in the final spinning process.

SAXONY WHEEL or FLAX WHEEL   This was the second type of spinning wheel which was driven by a foot pedal and had a flyer on the spindle, which enabled the spinning to be carried out as a continuous operation.

SCUTCHER   This was the machine developed soon after 1800 for cleaning the dirt out of the cotton after it had passed through the devil. It also rolled the cotton up into a lap ready for the carding engine.

SELVAGE   The edge or border of a piece of woven cloth. The warp threads in it are often thicker than in the rest of the cloth so it forms a strong edging.

SLIVER   An untwisted rope of fibres which stick together only through their own roughness. It has no strength and is easily broken.

SOUGH   This is an underground tunnel used for draining mines inside a hill.

STAPLE LENGTH   The length of the individual fibres of cotton or wool. Each type of cotton will have a different characteristic length.

STOCK CARDS   These were like hand cards but much larger, and were sometimes fixed to a table.

THROSTLE   This was an improved waterframe which had metal framing and cast iron gears so all the spindles and rollers could be driven by a set of gearing placed at one end.

THROWING   The term used for twisting the long strands or filaments of silk together.

WARP   This is the first set of threads or yarn placed in a loom which stretch from the back to the front. When they are properly entered and fixed, the loom is ready for weaving.

WATERFRAME   This was the term given to the spinning machine developed by Arkwright because it was driven by waterpower at Cromford. It had a wooden frame on which the spindles and rollers were grouped in sets of four, each set with its own gearing.

WEFT   This is the second set of threads put in a piece of cloth when weaving. The shuttle, as it is driven across the loom from side to side, leaves a trail of weft behind it which must then be beaten up by the reed.

WORSTED   A special type of wool cloth made from long fibres from which the shorter ones have been combed out. This gives a very smooth yarn so the cloth does not become "fluffy".

YARN   This is a single spun thread straight off the spinning machine. A length pulled off a bobbin will tend to untwist itself and form snarls.

Index

Picture Credits

The author and publishers wish to thank all those who have given permission for copyright illustrations to appear on the following pages: National Portrait Gallery, *frontispiece;* Science Museum, 8, 15, 16–17, 18 (top), 20 (bottom), 21, 28, 29 (bottom), 57; Ronan Picture Library, 10, 12, 12–13 (top), 26, 31, 42, 56; Mary Evans Picture Library, 18 (bottom), 20 (top), 29 (top), 48, 54, 59, 61, 65, 71, 72–73, 74, 77, 80, 81; Mansell collection, 58; Paul Popper, 60–61, 76, 83; British Museum, 8. Other pictures appear by permission of the author.